50

SIMPLE[...]
YOU CA[...]
TO DISASTER-PROOF
YOUR FINANCES

ALSO BY ILYCE GLINK

50 Simple Things You Can Do to Improve Your Personal Finances

100 Questions Every First-Time Home Buyer Should Ask

100 Questions You Should Ask About Your Personal Finances

10 Steps to Home Ownership

100 Questions Every Home Seller Should Ask

50 SIMPLE STEPS YOU CAN TAKE TO DISASTER-PROOF YOUR FINANCES

How to Plan Ahead to Protect Yourself and Your Loved Ones and Survive Any Crisis

Ilyce R. Glink

THREE RIVERS PRESS

NEW YORK

This book is intended as a general guide to the topics discussed, and it does not deliver accounting, personal finance, or legal advice. It is not intended, and should not be used, as a substitute for professional advice (legal or otherwise). You should consult a competent attorney, financial or estate planner, tax advisor, or other professionals with specific issues, problems, or questions you may have.

Company names, logos, and trademarks used in the book belong to the companies that own them. There is no attempt to appropriate these names, logos, and trademarks, and none should be construed. Also, there is no endorsement, implied or otherwise, of the companies listed in this book. They are used to illustrate the types of places, software, or information centers where readers can find more information. Finally, company names, phone numbers, addresses, and Web sites may have changed since the publication of this book.

If you wish to contact Ilyce R. Glink, visit her Web site, www.thinkglink.com.

Copyright © 2002 by Ilyce R. Glink

Published by Three Rivers Press, New York, New York.

Member of The Crown Publishing Group, a division of Random House, Inc.

www.randomhouse.com

THREE RIVERS PRESS and the Tugboat design are registered trademarks of Random House, Inc.

Printed in the United States of America

Library of Congress Cataloging-in-Publication Data
Glink, Ilyce R., 1964–
    50 simple steps you can take to disaster-proof your finances : how to plan ahead to protect yourself and your loved ones and survive any crisis / Ilyce R. Glink.
        p. cm.
    Includes index.
    1. Finance, Personal.   I. Title: Fifty simple steps you can take to disaster-proof your finances.   II. Title.
HG179 .G5518 2002
332.024'01—dc21   2002024686

ISBN 0-609-80995-4

10 9 8 7 6 5 4 3 2 1

First Edition

For my mother, Susanne, and my friend Pam,
both of whom survived financially intact,
but more important, with style and grace

Contents

CHAPTER 3 Travel

CHAPTER 4 Insurance and Health

CHAPTER 5 Investments

CHAPTER 6 Family Matters

CHAPTER 7 Estate Matters

CHAPTER 8 After the Disaster

Preface

As we all know, bad things happen to good people. Every day, people lose their jobs, are diagnosed with a terminal illness, or die. Fires destroy homes and offices. Rivers overflow and sweep away a lifetime of memories. Earthquakes crack open the earth, swallowing entire homes in an instant. And in a brief moment, life changes from the ordinary and expected, to something that is unfamiliar, scary, and devastating.

Disasters happen. They will wreak emotional havoc. But they don't have to disrupt your financial life. Just because the unthinkable has happened to you, either in your personal or professional life, doesn't mean your finances have to suffer the same fate. By preparing your finances to withstand the worst kinds of crisis, you may be able to devote more time afterward to recovering emotionally at a time when the hard work of managing your money—your security—may be beyond you.

I've wanted to write a book like this for a long time. I watched my mother, Susanne K. Glink, survive the sudden death of my father the week after my eighteenth birthday. She and my father had no real savings, retirement or otherwise. Fortunately, he had some life insurance, and after his death she received some money from the law firm where he had been a partner. It wasn't enough to pay for a lifetime of dreams, but it was a start. A year after my father died, my mother went to work as a real estate agent and became successful enough to provide my sisters and me with everything she'd always hoped to give us when she was a married, stay-at-home mom.

The other person I thought of often while writing this book was my friend Harry, who died along with two of his three children during a freak boating accident one beautiful, calm August day on Lake Michigan. Harry had created a plan—just in case—that would provide for his widow, Pam, and their children. The plan wasn't perfect when he died at the age of thirty-nine, but it was essentially in place. And in the years since this tragedy, it has allowed Pam and her son George to continue to live in their house and to do the things Pam feels are necessary to heal and move forward. It will continue to provide for them throughout the rest of their lives.

Life is full of curve balls. *50 Simple Steps You Can Take to Disaster-Proof Your Finances* is a way for you to step to the plate armed with the strongest bat you have. I hope you use this book as a game plan for preparing for the worst life has to offer. Your goal here isn't just to survive any crisis, but to thrive. Fill in the worksheets and keep this book in a safe, easily accessible place (perhaps even the home safe I suggest you purchase). Make sure you update it as your financial life changes.

This book won't stop bad things from happening, but it will keep you from suffering a tremendous financial loss on top of the personal or emotional losses you'll deal with in the event of a family crisis. And that peace of mind is priceless.

Ilyce R. Glink

PS: If you'd like to share your own survival stories, or if you just have a question, contact me through my Web site, www.thinkglink.com.

Introduction

When we're young, it's easy to believe we're immortal. But the older we get, the more fragile life appears. Bad things start to happen to people we know, older relatives, friends, someone or something we love. Some people have so many bad things happen, we begin to wonder if they aren't leading a cursed life. But for most of us, bad things happen only occasionally, and only once in a great while does disaster strike.

What is a disaster? It's easy to think of acts of terrorism or war, and the casualties that result. But we feel the pain of personal disasters much more—the sudden, unexpected death of a spouse, partner, parent, child, sibling, or close friend. A fire that breaks out one night while you're on vacation, killing the family dog and destroying your house. A shift in the earth that opens a sinkhole, swallowing your home in a matter of minutes. A flood that sweeps away a business or office. A recession that costs you and/or your spouse one or both jobs in a matter of months. Or perhaps a terminal illness that strikes you or a loved one.

When disaster strikes, it usually falls to one individual to pick up the pieces. Typically, one family member is assigned the bill paying, insurance buying, and money management duties. So when the crisis hits, you have a fifty-fifty chance that the one who is left behind can't find the checkbook and doesn't know where the insurance papers are.

Take a moment and imagine the worst thing that could happen to you or your family. Getting fired? Losing your home or office? The death of a partner or child? What would be the financial consequences? Would you take a small hit and recover quickly? Or would your family be left bereft emotionally and financially?

When a crisis happens, you won't be able to stop the emotional fallout. But you can do a few simple things in advance that will help you protect yourself and your loved ones from the financial fallout.

The unspoken bonus is that all of the tips and strategies I've put together for you in this book will not only help you disaster-proof your finances, but many of them will make your life easier day to day. Organizing your financial and personal life makes it a snap to take care of some of the more mundane realities, saving time and aggravation.

One more thought. Disaster-proofing your finances isn't something you do once and forget—well, you could, but eventually what you've planned wouldn't be as effective. That's because things change. You'll need to take stock of your disaster-planning at least once a year, or if a major change occurs. For example, if you buy a new home or put on a major addition, you'll need to update your homeowner's insurance. If you have another child, you'll want to change the beneficiaries on your life insurance. Keeping your disaster-proofing as current as possible should be your goal.

Let's get going.

— 1 —
Getting Organized

KEEP A CALENDAR
OF DAILY EVENTS UPDATED

Keeping things organized is a necessary first step toward protecting your family and your assets. Good organization starts with a daily calendar of events.

There are several reasons why you should have a calendar of daily events. The first is to know what you're doing and when. A detailed calendar saves you time and money, because you don't forget to do important things. Listing daily activities tells you where everyone is at any time. For example, if it's a Wednesday at 4:00 P.M. your children might be at soccer practice or their music lesson. You're at your office. Your spouse or partner has a meeting from 3:30 P.M. to 5:30 P.M. near your home.

If you know where everyone is all the time, or at least have a general sense of what they're doing, it's easy to develop a routine that friends and members of your extended family recognize. In case of an emergency, people will know where to find you. Clearly, cell phones and pagers help, too, but there are times when those useful pieces of technology are turned off, or they don't work, so it's helpful to know your family members' or friends' routines.

You probably already have a paper or printed calendar posted in the kitchen or some other high-traffic area so everyone in the family can see it. That's a fine start, but make sure everyone in the family consults it daily and at the beginning of each week. Often, one adult in the family is the "calendar keeper" and the other adult is clueless. Make sure the schedule is everyone's business.

Consider posting your daily events to electronic calendars as well. A Palm Pilot or another hand-held electronic calendar will allow every adult to keep track of the family daily doings, as well as all of your important phone numbers and notes about each person listed in the phone book. (Don't forget to include an address, phone number, and directions for each event.) You can block out for years to come annual events like birthdays, anniversaries, and holidays. You can also include a lot of information about each event, including the address, phone numbers, and other details. If your Palm is linked to your computer, you can print up a daily, weekly, or monthly calendar and distribute it. You can also keep a "To Do" list.

Another option is to post your family calendar on a Web site like Yahoo!, which allows anyone with the password to log on from anywhere in the world and check on what's happening with you or your family. If you use Yahoo!'s calendar or another Web-based calendar, you can update it from anywhere in the world as well. That makes it easy to change dates from, say, the office, or home, or the business center of a hotel halfway around the world.

A GOOD START

At the beginning of each year, write all of your important dates into your calendar. Certainly, you'll want to include birthdays, anniversaries, holidays, vacations, and dates with friends, but more important, write down dates of financial consequence. For example, if you're self-employed, you might mark down the dates you owe the IRS your estimated taxes. If you're employed by a company, you might want to check on your withholding on October 1, to give yourself enough time to make any necessary adjustments so you don't overpay the government.

Consider this checklist a place to start, especially if you're self-employed.

January 15: Estimated tax due (for self-employed individuals).

February 1: Deadline to send your tax information to your accountant or tax preparer.

March 15: Tax day for corporations (if your business is set up as a corporation and works on a calendar year); last day to make contributions to retirement plans for the previous year.

April 15: Tax day for individuals; last day to make contributions to IRA, Roth IRA, for the previous year. Estimated tax due (for self-employed individuals).

June 15: Estimated tax due (for self-employed individuals).

September 15: Estimated tax due (for self-employed individuals).

October 1: Check withholdings and adjust if necessary.

December 31: Last date to open an IRA, Roth IRA, Keogh, or SIMPLE plan for the current tax year.

You might also want to plug in the dates for your mortgage payments (typically the first of each month), credit card payments (you should remind yourself a week before they're due to allow time for the post office to deliver it, unless you pay electronically), school tuition bills, camp bills, and any other important financial dates.

Keep in mind when you're filling out your calendar that it's easy to get caught up in the minutiae of daily life. I want you to know specifically where your children are—at school from 9 to 3, and at soccer practice until 4, and then at a friend's house until 6 and then home again. You should also know fairly specifically where your spouse or partner is during the day (at the office, at the store, lunch meeting out, in court, or wherever).

But you don't need to account for every minute of someone's day. That's a little too controlling for most of us. It's more important to have a general understanding of a family member's daily routine. That way, if something does happen, you'll know where to call to try and reach someone.

KEEP YOUR PERSONAL
ADDRESS BOOK UPDATED

Most of our personal address books look like the one I recently threw out. A small, hard- or soft-cover book about the size of my hand, with so many cross-outs, white-outs, and new names taped or pasted or glued over old ones that it's difficult to know who lives where and what their phone number is. Indeed, with all of the new area codes (like 678, 954, 847), it's difficult to know whether you're even calling inside the United States!

If someone had to find a number in your address book in an emergency, could they even read the entries? Would they even know where to look for it? (Mine was in my home office, in a hanging file folder in a cabinet underneath my desk. Most of the time, I couldn't find it myself!)

Keeping an updated list of family and friends' numbers and addresses at home and at work is essential when a crisis erupts. When my father died in a small town in Michigan, I dialed telephone numbers I knew by heart. But in an emergency, memories fail, and important numbers may be out of reach. On September 11, 2001, my New York City editor realized that her address book, with the work numbers of all her siblings—including one who worked right next to the Pentagon—was at home. It took dozens of frantic relayed calls to track everyone down and reassure them she was safe.

She now has a complete set of emergency numbers at home and at work.

Keeping your telephone numbers in an electronic format is a good idea for all of the reasons discussed in Simple Step 1: It's easily accessed. You can keep much more information, including e-mail addresses, Web sites, mobile and pager numbers, addresses of several homes, faxes (in case you need to send important documents), and notes on what day your doctor has off. They're easy to update and you can print copies.

Electronic phone books allow you to organize and find the information in any number of ways. You can search by last name, first name, name of company, and date (if you choose something like a Palm Pilot, which has a calendar attached). You can also sort names and phone numbers into categories, such as family, friends, doctors, financial institutions, or whatever you like.

When you leave your home, you should either carry a Palm Pilot or another hand-held organizer with you that has your electronic telephone book on it, or a printout of your current phone list. Keep another printout at home, in an accessible place, and another copy in your home safe (see Simple Step 7). Update regularly.

A GOOD START

Declare "Address Amnesia/Amnesty Day," and send mass e-mails to family and friends asking them to verify and update all their important information. (While you're at it, admit you're a little fuzzy on your nephew's birthday and snag all those dates, too.)

In addition to keeping you organized, your electronic phone list has several satisfying uses, including giving you a big head start when you send holiday cards or invitations to parties.

On your computer, you can drag the addresses over and create mailing labels, which you can then run off on your printer. You can create return address labels and print them yourself, eliminating the need to rewrite your name over and over again.

For those who remain steadfastly opposed to all things electronic, consider starting a new address book, and using the return labels on friends' cards to keep it updated. Once your address book is updated, photocopy the pages so you can keep an extra copy at home and one with you at all times.

Again, there are several electronic address books—including Yahoo!, MSN.com, and at America Online—that will allow you to access your phone numbers from any computer. Ultimately, this may be your most flexible choice. I'm not concerned about someone hacking his or her way into your private information as long as you stick with the brand-name Web companies, such as these three. Privacy is crucial to keeping their clientele tuned in, and these companies have spent millions to ensure that your information is safe.

SIMPLE STEP

3

CONSTRUCT AN EMERGENCY
CONTACT LIST

Once you have your phone book updated, it's time to create a contact list of emergency names. Even if you have all of your phone numbers in one place, someone else looking at the list may not have the foggiest notion who these people are (unless you're using an electronic phone book and have filled in this information).

Your emergency contact list should include the following information:

- Your cell phone or pager numbers, and those of your spouse or partner or any other adult who lives in your household

- Your parents' names and numbers (including cell and pagers)

- Close friend or family member's name and numbers

- If divorced, name and numbers for your ex-spouse

- Doctors' names and numbers

- Dentist's name and number

- Attorney's name and number

- If you have children, school names, addresses, and numbers

- Names and numbers of your children's babysitters, or aging parents' care providers

- Service providers, including lawn care (if a tree or major limb comes down on your property), snow removal, cleaning help, pet care, veterinary and animal hospital, travel agency; also, health insurance carrier and the toll-free emergency number (many health insurance companies require you to call a toll-free number within twenty-four to thirty-six hours after being admitted for emergency care), and any necessary authorization numbers (for example, the employee number for your HMO)

- Other names and numbers of important people with whom you're in daily contact

Update this list every time a telephone number, address, or cell phone number changes. Date the list, so you know how recent it is. We keep our emergency phone list in a separate file on our computer because the information is so limited and specialized. This way, we can update it instantly and print out new copies.

My husband, Sam, keeps a copy of the list at his office, and I have a copy in my office. We have several copies posted in our home, including one in the drawer by the kitchen phone and one posted to the bulletin board on the other side of the kitchen, which is our family information clearinghouse (the usual collage of calendar, invitations, school lists and dates, and so on).

This is the list you might want to distribute to your family or close friends when you travel. In case of an emergency, your family will then know how to get in touch with each other and the professionals and service providers who help you every day.

My Emergency Contact List

Family Members/Friends

_____ Phone _____ Cell _____ Pager _____

_____ Phone _____ Cell _____ Pager _____

_____ Phone _____ Cell _____ Pager _____

_____ Phone _____ Cell _____ Pager _____

_____ Phone _____ Cell _____ Pager _____

_____ Phone _____ Cell _____ Pager _____

Neighbor _____ Address_____

Phone_____ Cell phone _____

Neighbor _____ Address_____

Phone_____ Cell phone _____

Police emergency <u>911</u>   Non emergency _____

Fire emergency <u>911</u>   Non emergency _____

Alarm company _____ Code _____

Medical & Insurance

Doctor _____ Phone _____

Address _____

Doctor _____ Phone _____

Address _____

Pediatrician _____ Phone _____

Address _____

Dentist_____ Phone _____

Address _____

Pediatric dentist _____ Phone _____

Address _____

Closest Hospital _____ Phone _____

Address _____

Health Insurance Company _____ Number_____

Insurance Number _____

Pharmacy_____ Phone _____

Address _____

Attorney _____ Phone _____
Address _____
Home insurance agent _____ Phone _____
Address _____

Schools

Child _____ School Name _____ Phone _____
Address _____
Child _____ School Name _____ Phone _____
Address _____
Child _____ School Name _____ Phone _____
Address _____

Service Providers

Babysitters _____ Number _____
Cleaning help_____ Number _____
Lawn service _____ Number _____
Snow removal_____ Number _____
Plumber_____ Number _____
Electrician _____ Number _____
Other _____ Number _____
Other _____ Number _____
Other _____ Number _____
Other _____ Number _____
Other _____ Number _____

A GOOD START

Use this worksheet as your phone list. You can either write in the book, or photocopy it to use over and over again.

CONSTRUCT A LIST OF ASSETS AND CONTACT NUMBERS

Knowing how to reach important friends, family members, doctors, school officials, and other service providers is a good step toward linking your daily life to your financial life. The next step is to create a list of assets, along with the addresses, phone numbers, Web sites, and other contact information. This list, which you'll update whenever there is a significant change in your assets (such as the purchase of a new insurance policy or when you open or close a bank account), should be kept at home in your home safe (see Simple Step 7), with a copy in your safe deposit box (see Simple Step 8). It's also a good idea to distribute the list to the attorney who prepared your wills or the executor of your estate (see Chapter 7).

What should your assets list include? Start with these items:

- All bank accounts, including savings, checking, and money market accounts

- All investment accounts (whether you hold mutual funds, individual stocks and bonds, or cash)

- All retirement accounts, including work-sponsored retirement accounts—401(k), 403(b), 457 plans—and self-directed IRAs, Keoghs, SEPs, and SIMPLE plans.

- All Roth IRA or rollover IRA accounts
- Any CDs, bonds, or stocks in which you rather than a financial institution hold the certificates (and where they are located)
- Policy numbers of any relevant insurance, including life insurance and disability policies. You might also include the name and number of your health, long-term care (if you have it), auto insurance, and other insurance policies
- Contact information for your accountant or tax preparer, attorney, executor of your estate, and financial planner, if you have one
- Mailboxes (post office boxes and any boxes at private mail companies)
- Safe deposit boxes, and where they're located

For each of these assets, write down the name of the bank or financial institution, as well as the address, phone number, Web site, and account numbers. For insurance policies, write down the name of the institution, phone number, and policy number. For individuals, write down their names, company, address, phone number, and e-mail address.

You may have assets that are not included on this list, such as a home, vacation home, rental or investment property, boats, cars, motorcycles, trailers, and perhaps an airplane. Be sure to keep the deeds or titles to these items up to date and clipped together in a safe place, like your safe deposit box.

You may also want to keep a list of the credit cards that you currently own. If you choose to add the credit cards to your list of assets, be sure to include the toll-free number that anyone can call to put a stop on your account, in case you can't do it yourself.

If it seems unsafe to list your credit card numbers with all of the rest of your financial information, then just list the banks that issue the credit card numbers, with the toll-free numbers. Make sure the names you use with the cards are indicated as well. You can keep copies of the actual numbers in your home safe or safe deposit box.

Business Owners

If you're self-employed or if you own a small business, it's smart to make a list of your business accounts and assets and to keep this list updated. Business owners will want to have a list of all accounts related to the business, including checking, savings, and money market accounts, as well as lines of credit, a client list, and accounts payable and receivable. Make sure you include all contact information for your business's accountant, attorney, and board of directors (if you have one).

A GOOD START

Use the following worksheet to keep a handle on your assets. Remember, update it as necessary.

Your List of Assets

Banks & Financial Institutions

Name of institution: _____ Acct. no. _____
Address _____ Phone_____ Web _____
Name of institution: _____ Acct. no. _____
Address _____ Phone_____ Web _____
Name of institution: _____ Acct. no. _____
Address _____ Phone_____ Web _____
Name of institution: _____ Acct. no. _____
Address _____ Phone_____ Web _____
Name of institution: _____ Acct. no. _____
Address _____ Phone_____ Web _____

Investment & Retirement Accounts

Name of institution: _____ Acct. no. _____
Address _____ Phone_____ Web _____
Name of institution: _____ Acct. no. _____
Address _____ Phone_____ Web _____
Name of institution: _____ Acct. no. _____
Address _____ Phone_____ Web _____
Name of institution: _____ Acct. no. _____
Address _____ Phone_____ Web _____
Name of institution: _____ Acct. no. _____
Address _____ Phone_____ Web _____

CDs, Stocks & Bonds (Held by you in a safe deposit box)

Asset _____ Location _____
Asset _____ Location _____
Asset _____ Location _____
Asset _____ Location _____
Asset _____ Location _____

Real Estate, and Other Real Property

Asset _____ Location of property documents*_____
Asset _____ Location of property documents _____
Asset _____ Location of property documents _____
Asset _____ Location of property documents _____
Asset _____ Location of property documents _____

Insurance Policies

Life insurance company _____ Policy no. _____
Phone number _____
Life insurance company _____ Policy no. _____
Phone number _____
Life insurance company _____ Policy no. _____
Phone number _____
Long-term care_____ Policy no. _____
Phone number _____
Health insurance company _____ Policy no. _____
Phone number _____
Auto insurance company _____ Policy no. _____
Phone number _____
Umbrella coverage _____ Policy no. _____
Phone number _____
Business insurance _____ Policy no. _____
Phone number _____
Homeowner's insurance _____ Policy no. _____
Phone number _____
Disability insurance _____ Policy no. _____
Phone number _____
Other insurance _____ Policy no. _____
Phone number _____

---

*Property documents include deed, note or mortgage, and the title insurance policy.

Professionals

Attorney _____ Phone no. _____

Address _____ e-mail _____

Accountant _____ Phone no. _____

Address _____ e-mail _____

Financial planner _____ Phone no. _____

Address _____ e-mail _____

Other _____ Phone no. _____

Address _____ e-mail _____

Safe deposit box _____ Phone no. _____

Credit card _____ Phone no. _____

Credit card _____ Phone no. _____

Credit card _____ Phone no. _____

Credit card _____ Phone no. _____

Credit card _____ Phone no. _____

Major jewelry/artwork _____

_____

_____

_____

Car _____ Year _____

VIN _____ License plate _____

Car _____ Year _____

VIN _____ License plate _____

Car _____ Year _____

VIN _____ License plate _____

Other vehicle _____ Year _____

VIN _____ License plate _____

Boat _____ Year _____

Model number _____ Registration _____

Inventory of major house purchases

_____

_____

_____

_____

_____

KEEP YOUR IMPORTANT DOCUMENTS CLOSE AT HAND

In a crisis, having the right documents handy will be critical to making your life run as smoothly as possible while your emotional life is in turmoil. Having the wrong documents, or not being able to put your hands on the right documents, could mean a delay in getting an insurance payout, gaining access to a safe deposit box, or having an IRA or other retirement account roll over to the beneficiaries.

What documents are important? The following list will help you construct an all-important paper trail that will make it much easier to reconstruct your financial life in the event of a disaster:

Important Documents

Insurance policies: life, auto, health, disability, long-term care, umbrella liability, homeowner's

Estate documents: including copies of your will, living will, power of attorney for health care, power of attorney for financial matters, and any trust documents (see Chapter 7)

Bank account statements: you only need a copy of one statement for each account from each institution, updated once a year. A year-end statement would work.

Retirement accounts: a copy of one statement for each account, from each institution, updated once a year. A year-end statement is helpful.

Most recent tax return

Copies of the titles or leases to real estate, cars, boats, and planes

Copies of stocks and bonds that you hold

Loan documents: mortgages, school debt, auto loans, personal loans, business loans

Warranties for big-ticket items

Home purchase/sale and capital improvement records: especially if the potential profit on your home exceeds $250,000 for single homeowners and $500,000 for married homeowners

Credit card statements: a copy of one statement per account, updated every time you cancel or add a card

Other investment information

Important contracts, including employment and partnership agreements

Copyrights, patents, and trademarks

Title insurance policies for your home or other properties

Social security cards, birth certificates, and death certificates

Driver's license or state ID card

Passport

Visa (if you are not a citizen of the U.S.) or green card

Marriage certificate, divorce decree, judgments, etc.

Child adoption papers, child custody agreement

Funeral arrangements: plot documentation, receipt for funeral if yours is already planned and paid for

A GOOD START

Start by collecting all of your important documents. Then make three copies of all of them. Put the originals into a flat folder. Since you'll keep your originals in your safe deposit box, you'll want the folder to be as flat and compact as possible. The idea is to keep the originals out of your home, so they won't be destroyed in a fire or flood.

Take a second set of your most important documents and put them into another folder, perhaps a three-ring binder with pockets or room for three-hole plastic folders. Slip one set of copies into the folder and put it in your home safe.

Ask the estate attorney who prepared your estate plan (including your will, living will, and powers of attorney for health care and financial matters) to hang on to your third (and optional) set of important documents.

Depending on the crisis, you may need additional paperwork, including a death certificate, employment contract (if you have one), or copies of other work contracts. If solving a financial problem relies on one of these documents, include them in your important documents file.

Small Business Owners

If you own a small business, or are partners with other investors in real estate, you'll need to protect the documents that are important to defining the scope, ownership, and finances of the business, including corporate organizational documents and your incorporation documents.

Make sure you collect and photocopy important documents, including partnership and corporation documents, business bank and investment accounts, business credit cards, work ID or security cards, tax returns, succession plans, and documents detailing ownership of business assets, including real property, cars, and planes.

When Tony died suddenly, his widow, Lucy, fell apart. Not only did she have to recover from the emotional loss of her husband, and the father of their children, but she had to spend time fighting her husband's partner over the fair valuation of their business.

While Tony had told Lucy that he and Randy split everything 50/50, Randy said he actually owned 75 percent of the business. He told Lucy that he had put up all the money for the business and that Tony had said he'd get everything in case he died.

But Lucy didn't think that was the case, and she was sure that Tony and Randy had a partnership agreement. She and her attorney searched through several boxes of documents in Tony's basement office and finally found the original partnership agreement. Not only was Randy lying, but it was Tony who had put up most of the money and owned 75 percent of the business.

Since Lucy had inherited everything under Tony's will, she and her attorney got an independent appraiser to value the business. Because she was able to find the partnership agreement that had been signed by both Tony and Randy (and Randy was unable to provide any documentation that backed up his claims), she was able to get Randy to pay a substantial sum of money for Tony's share of the business.

Having important documents doesn't mean much if your spouse or partner can't find them when they need to.

Keep one set of your important documents on site, perhaps in an office safe, and another set off-site, either in a business safe deposit box or with your company attorney.

SIMPLE STEP
6

BACK UP YOUR COMPUTER FILES

How many times have you been working on a document, only to have your computer freeze on you? Or, opted not to "save" because you thought you had just saved, only to realize you just deleted something you'd never saved? Either way, it's enormously frustrating because you've lost not only whatever it is you were working on, but the time it will take to reconstruct it.

Although it's been drilled into our heads to save our documents every few minutes, not many of us do that. We rely on auto-backup programs and sophisticated software to do the work for us.

The only problem with that is, sometimes they don't work.

For most consumers, backing up computer information will mostly entail backing up Quicken, Microsoft Money, or whatever financial software program you use. You'll want to make sure that your financial information is as safe as possible. You might also want to back up documents, including letters or the electronic diary you've been keeping for your children. As the technology gets better, more consumers will have digital photos and video on their home computers, which they'd rather not lose; you'll want copies of those, too.

For an easy, cheap (always a plus!) way to back up your

computer, buy a CD-rewrite drive (also known as CD-RW). These handy devices "burn" a copy of your entire hard drive (or just your most frequently used information) onto a CD in a matter of minutes. Not only can you back up your system, but you can then take it with you and use it in your laptop. (Remember, once you've "burned" your CD, you can't add or delete information to it. You can't "reburn" a CD.)

But that's okay. Inexpensive stacks of 100 CD-RWs are available at Sam's Club, Costco, and any computer or office supply warehouse. If you get in the habit of "burning" a new CD every week or so, your computer system will never be more than a week out of date.

A GOOD START

Like most computer products, CD-rewrite drives are getting simultaneously faster and cheaper. When they were first introduced, they cost hundreds of dollars and were very slow. Now, you can pay just $69 for a CD-rewrite drive system that is six times as fast as the system introduced a year earlier.

Another nice feature is that you don't have to be a computer genius to install the CD-rewrite drive or the accompanying software.

Watch the Sunday ads in your local newspaper for sales at Best Buy, Circuit City, Comp USA, and other computer stores. If you get lucky, you might find a CD-rewrite on sale with a rebate from the manufacturer.

Once you have the system installed, make sure you buy a stack of blank CDs. Then pick one day a week to back up your system. Be sure to deposit your backup CD-ROM in your house safe or your safe deposit box (or both).

Small Business Owners

Business owners should back up their systems at least once a week. If you have a tremendous amount of information going into your system that would be impossible to duplicate, you may want to back up your system more frequently, perhaps every day. To avoid losing your information, be sure to keep a backup copy of your records in a location separate and distinct from your office environment. You can keep it at your home, in a safe deposit box located in a bank, or at your attorney's or tax preparer's office. Just make sure that it's protected in case the unthinkable happens—such as an entire neighborhood wiped out due to a fire, flood, or earthquake.

SIMPLE STEP

7

RENT A SAFE DEPOSIT BOX

A safe deposit box is literally a box located in a vault at a bank. The vault itself will probably look like something out of the old hit TV series, *Get Smart*, with heavy steel doors behind another set of fireproof doors, behind a third or even fourth set of (hopefully) fireproof, bombproof doors. It may even be located on the lower level of your bank.

Safe deposit boxes are supposed to be a safe place to put important, irreplaceable documents (such as your estate documents, stock and bond certificates, deeds and insurance policies), valuables (such as gold and silver coins, or jewelry), backup CDs of your computer information, and other stuff you'd rather hang on to, like old photographs, birth certificates, and your grandparents' marriage license.

While safe deposit boxes can be broken into or melted in a fire, the odds are that yours is going to be just fine. Also, it's extremely unlikely that something will happen to your safe deposit box at the same time something catastrophic happens to your home.

The only negatives to a safe deposit box are the actual cost of renting one and the fact that you have to have a key to get into it (this is a security precaution as well). If you choose a safe deposit box that's difficult to get to, you can add inconvenience to the list.

The annual rental cost of a safe deposit box ranges from

free (I was offered a free safe deposit box for life when I was one of the first customers at a new bank in my hometown) to $50 to more than $1,000 for a safe deposit box big enough for a Renoir painting.

Keys are another problem, especially if you lose them. Typically, you're given two keys to a safe deposit box. If you lose one, you'll probably have to pay a fee to the bank when you decide to stop leasing the box. If you lose both keys, it could cost you several hundred dollars to have the bank break into your box and change the hardware. The bank keeps a copy of its own key to the box, but not your key— and typically two keys are needed to get into the box.

Many consumers are surprised to find out that their bank or financial institution limits its liability if something should happen to your safe deposit box. In many cases, if your safe deposit box is melted during an intense fire, or if the contents are ruined in a flood, the bank or financial institution has limited liability or no liability. So if your important documents are ruined, and your grandmother's gold and pearl wedding ring is destroyed, you won't get restitution from the bank. You'll need to insure these items yourself. But it's important to check out the liability policy when you rent your safe deposit box, so you understand what the risks are.

A GOOD START

Make a list of two or three banks that are reasonably close to either your home or where you work. If you seem to change jobs or move fairly frequently, choose your location carefully. While you can close a safe deposit box and rent another one elsewhere, it'll take at a minimum a few hours to open a new box, close the old one, and move your valuables.

Call the banks on your list and price out the safe deposit boxes. Look at how much the banks are charging for different size boxes, then think about how much space you really need. I started out with the smallest size box, and then when the new bank in town opened, I "graduated" to a larger box that could accommodate more paperwork. Be sure to check the times and days of the week that you can access your box. While most banks allow you to access your box from 9:00 A.M. to 5:00 P.M., Monday through Friday, others may have more limited hours. If that's a consideration, or if you need your box to be available to you early in the morning or late at night, be sure to find a bank that has flexible hours.

Finally, look around for new banks that may have special deals, like the one I took advantage of. If a safe deposit box costs you fifty dollars per year, and you can open up a checking account in a new bank and get your box for free forever, or for five dollars, that's a big savings. Just make sure you're not required to keep copious amounts of cash in that checking account (without any interest!) in order to get the safe deposit box "for free."

2

Banking and Credit

BUY A HOME SAFE

While a safe deposit box will keep your valuables and important documents safe outside of your home, it's helpful to have a safe place within your home to store cash, copies of your important documents, and valuable jewelry when it's not being worn. Perhaps the best part about a home safe is that it protects your valuables in case of a fire and, if you bolt it into the wall or floor of your basement (or another room), excellent protection against theft as well.

There are a variety of different types of safes, and you can spend a whole lot of money buying protection you'll never need. Here are the basic types, according to Glavin Security Specialists, a fifty-year-old company that provides security to some of the top companies and buildings in Chicago:

High-security safes: These are commercial safes most often bought by banks, jewelers, retail stores, parking lots, and currency exchanges. Depending on the business, an insurance company may require a company to purchase this type of safe in order to be able to purchase commercial insurance. This safe offers the maximum security against fire (typically up to 1500° Fahrenheit) and every known method of entry.

Medium-security safes: These safes offer security against fire and burglary, but they are not as thick and strong as the safes you might find inside a bank. That's fine, because for most families, under most conditions, these safes will give you the kind of protection you're looking for.

Floor safes: If you're just building a home or if you're pouring a new basement floor, you might consider buying and installing a floor safe. When buried in the floor and surrounded by concrete, these safes offer almost the same protection as high-security safes. Floor safes, even without being embedded in concrete, still offer a high degree of protection against burglary.

Fire safes: These safes are designed to provide maximum protection for documents in the event of a fire, as well as adequate protection from the average burglar (that is, someone who hasn't made it a life's work cracking safes). A fire safe has an inner lining made out of fire clay. When fire clay is heated in a fire, it releases steam into a container. The steam helps keep a fire from starting inside the safe chamber when the temperatures rise from the fire. If you decide to install a fire safe, the manufacturer will suggest that you keep your documents in a plastic sealed bag to prevent damage due to excessive moisture.

Self-contained locking device safes: A relatively new type of safe, these will eliminate the time and difficulty of a mechanical combination lock. The safes use a quick-access touch keypad and can be opened with a six-digit combination in about seven seconds. In addition, combinations can be easily changed, giving you more control of your security. A built-in antitheft device will institute a three-minute lockout period once five incorrect combinations have been entered into the keypad.

A GOOD START

When figuring out which safe to buy think about how much stuff you're going to keep in the safe at any one time, where you're going to put it, what sorts of risks the safe might face, and how much you want to spend.

You can purchase a safe from a private security company or through office supply companies. Online office supply companies have cheaper safes starting at fifty dollars, and these may be fine for home use. The fifty-dollar chest is small, but it will protect your valuables and documents for up to a half hour in a 1500° Fahrenheit blaze. But the safe weighs only nineteen pounds, so unless you bolt it to the floor somehow, someone could just pick it up and walk away with it. A safe advertised for $600 weighs 290 pounds, and in addition to offering premium fireproof protection, is built with four five-eighth-inch dead bolts for additional security. The lock has one million possible combinations.

Again, think about how many things you might store in your safe and where you might keep it before you buy one. I ended up spending around $200 for a medium-size safe that offered good fire protection coupled with the ability to bolt it into the floor.

Small Business Owners

To protect important or irreplaceable files or documents in your home or office, you may want to purchase a fireproof filing cabinet, offered by office supply companies, in addition to an office safe.

Office supply companies offer more than three dozen different types of fireproof filing cabinets. One company's Web site offers a 25-inch deep, vertical fireproof filing cabinet, with a steel-lattice reinforcement that can withstand a fall from thirty feet (just in case you need to drop it out of a third-story window). The manufacturer says steel-lined insulation makes each drawer a separate fireproof container. The filing cabinet has a high enough rating that it should survive a fire of up to 1700° Fahrenheit for up to one hour. Every part of the cabinet is warrantied against failure for as long as you own it.

The cost for fireproof filing cabinets runs between $700 and $2,000, depending on the size and fireproof strength of the cabinet. The best thing about the cabinet is that it looks like all of your other filing cabinets, so you can place it anywhere in your office or a closet and have it blend in with everything else.

ALWAYS KEEP CASH AROUND

When I was a teenager going out with friends or even on a date, my parents would remind me to carry a little extra cash—"mad money," they called it. In case something didn't work out right, or my friends and I had a fight and I decided to leave, I'd have the means to get home safely.

These were the days before just about everyone had a cell phone, pager, Blackberry, or some other form of electronic communication. And rarely did anyone under the age of twenty-one carry a credit card. The closest thing you might have had was a department store or gas credit card.

Today it's easier to get in touch and it's easier to pay for things even if you're not carrying a wad of greenbacks. Most kids carry ATM cards, which allow them to withdraw cash at millions of stations (perhaps paying a buck or two in fees, but that's worth it in an emergency). Or they carry debit cards, a "fake" Visa or MasterCard that looks like a credit card but acts like a checkbook—though without all of the benefits or consumer protections of a real credit card.

But the concept of "mad money" is still important, especially in a crisis. Instead of needing twenty dollars to get you home in a taxi, you might need $20,000 to pay all of your bills for two, three, or four months, until you receive a life insurance check, or your long-term disability benefits kick in, or the marital accounts are unfrozen, or you get your child support checks.

Of course, you don't need to keep all of that cash under your mattress. (I'll talk about the benefits of an emergency fund in Simple Step 10.) But having a few hundred dollars in cash in your home safe can allow you to maximize your time and money.

First, if you need emergency cash—to pay for a taxi to the hospital, or if you run short with the babysitter—it's a lot easier to go to your home safe for the cash than it is to drive to the closest ATM. Also, keeping cash on hand allows you to go to the bank once a week or once every other week, instead of making multiple trips, or perhaps stopping at an ATM that's outside of your network and paying a fee. Finally, if you're going on a trip, you can use your home safe to store your traveler's checks and currency until you leave for the airport (and passports, travel visas, tickets, travel insurance policies, etc.).

Keeping some cash in your pocket can be extremely useful—unless you're one of those folks who has no self-control. If you find that you're spending every dollar you can get your hands on, then keep as little cash in your pocket as possible.

A GOOD START

How much cash should you keep on hand? Start the calculations by writing down how much cash you and your family go through in a given week. I'm not talking about total expenditures, including checks, credit cards, and debit cards, but cold hard cash.

For example, do you pay a cleaning lady twice a week? Do you give your children a weekly allowance, plus another few bucks on the weekend? Do you pay cash for your bus or train tokens or pass cards each week? Do you have a babysitter for your children on the weekends? Do you shop for your groceries with cash? Pay for meals at work, coffee in the morning, dry cleaning on the way home from work?

Let's say you go through $250 in cash each week. You'll probably want to keep $500 to $750 in cash just to make sure that you'll have enough in the event you can't get to a cash machine or the bank in the middle of a crisis. Plan on having two or three times your weekly cash outlay in your safe—just in case.

Small Businesses

Keeping a small amount of petty cash in an office is fine. But when you get into serious sums of money, it's easy for that cash to disappear, especially if someone else knows the combination to the safe.

If your business is a cash business, you'll need to take extra precautions to avoid losing cash (which is difficult to insure) in a fire or flood. Consider buying a bank-grade safe with the best fireproofing materials, or hiring a security firm to help you protect your cash in the event of an emergency.

SIMPLE STEP
10

BUILD A SUBSTANTIAL
EMERGENCY SAVINGS ACCOUNT

There's nothing like a fat bank account to make you sleep better at night. And if you know that your nest egg will get you through any crisis, you'll feel even better.

But how much do you really need to feel comfortable if something happens? That depends. If you're trying to soothe yourself emotionally after a devastating loss, such as the death of your spouse or child, or losing everything in a fire or flood, no amount of money will suffice. But if you're trying to get through the day, paying all of your regular bills and some new ones, then it's easier to figure out how much to have in your emergency account.

Before we start calculating, let's just be clear: The amount you need to have in your emergency fund account, at a bank or other financial institution, is *in addition to* the cash you ought to have in your pocket or your house safe. Your emergency fund is there to provide for all of your ongoing expenses, including mortgage, real estate taxes, insurance, education, federal income taxes, and so on. The cash in your safe is meant to tide you over if your wallet and all of your credit cards get lost or stolen.

Most financial planners recommend you keep anywhere from three to six months' worth of expenses in a savings account. The idea is that if you lose your job, or your spouse dies or goes on long-term disability, you'll have money in the bank to pay your bills.

But even if the worst does happen, you won't need all that cash at once. So instead of leaving your cash in an account in which it earns virtually (or actually) nothing, one option might be to keep one or two months' worth of expenses in the savings account and the rest in a short-term certificate of deposit (CD), which ought to pay better. While your money will be "tied up" for four weeks at a time (you can roll over the CD when it comes due), you'll earn more money on your money, and with the cash in your savings account you shouldn't come up short at the end of the month.

A GOOD START

If you've never kept track of your monthly or annual expenses, it's about time you tried. The easiest way to do this is by purchasing either Quicken or Microsoft Money software, and keeping track of your finances online. Or you can do it the low-tech way and purchase a small notebook, writing down every cent you spend during the weeks and months.

Knowing how much your life costs you is essential information in planning for a crisis. It can help you gauge how much insurance you need to purchase, what kind of estate plan you need, and how much you should keep safe in your emergency fund.

Use the following worksheet to help jog your memory about how much you spend each week, month, and year. Then start keeping track of your expenses, either electronically or with paper and pen, going forward.

How Much Do You Spend?
Worksheet

Item	Week	Month	Year
Savings			
Mortgage			
Federal/state income taxes			
Real estate taxes			
Life insurance			
Homeowner's insurance			
Car insurance			
Other insurance			
Home maintenance			
Condo/homeowner assoc. dues			
Utilities			
Food/drugstore items			
Clothing/dry cleaners			
Nanny/babysitters			
Medical insurance			
Medical costs			
Health club			
Entertainment (books/movies/ CDs/nights out)			
Recreation			
Travel/vacations			
Education/tuition			
Auto expenses (gas, repairs, parking fees)			
Auto loan(s)			
School loan(s)			
Credit card debt			
Personal loans			
Lunch/dinner out			
Takeout			
Gifts			
Children's miscellaneous			
Miscellaneous			
Total			

Once you know how much you spend, it will be easy for you to start eliminating some of the "nonessential" expenses in order to start your emergency fund (you're going for enough cash to cover three to six months of expenses). For example, instead of buying dozens of holidays gifts in December, consider making gifts and banking the difference. Or you could make a small donation in a family member's name to a worthwhile charity. There are lots of ways of giving without spending a lot of cash. For instance, give someone a one-year subscription to their favorite magazine. It will be relatively inexpensive for you, but your friend or relative will remember your thoughtfulness throughout the year. To save more, eat out less often, and bank the difference. Fire the lawn service and do your own yard work (your heart and waistline will thank you).

Another way to build your emergency fund is to save your change. Every night, empty your pockets or change purse of the change you've accumulated throughout the day—plus your lowest denomination bill. If you can manage to save two dollars per day, you'll save nearly $725 for your emergency fund. If you save $100 per month, or about three dollars per day, you'll have $1,000 in the kitty by the end of the year.

Since I started writing my syndicated column in 1993, I've heard from many readers who have had trouble getting through a crisis simply because they never thought about setting aside some emergency cash.

Here's how it happens. Just as they're starting to save a little money, the car breaks down and needs major work ($950), or the kids need to go to the doctor or dentist ($100), or the roof starts leaking and needs to be fixed ($600). Some legitimate need always seems to eat away at the emergency fund.

The problem with that is you never get ahead. You never get to a place financially that allows you a little breathing room, a small cushion in case disaster strikes.

Brenda wrote to me from Atlanta. A few months after her baby was born, her husband Bob got into a terrible car accident. They had finally managed to pay off their credit card debt, though they still had school loans and a car loan. But Bob was out of work for six months. The driver of the car that hit him was uninsured. His car insurance paid for the damage and most of the medical bills (his insurance premium, predictably, went up the next year). But there were other bills that weren't covered.

In fact, Brenda and Bob went through all of their savings and ran up another $10,000 in debt while he recovered from the accident. Without their savings and a little help from her parents, they might have been $20,000 in debt.

SIMPLE STEP
11

KEEP UP WITH YOUR BILLS

When disaster strikes, many of the ordinary, regular things you do every day—like opening the mail—simply won't get done. Quite possibly, you won't examine your bank statements or balance your checkbook. You may forget to deposit or cash your paychecks. You may even forget to pay your bills.

If you go a month or so without paying your bills, nothing drastic will happen. However, if you forget to pay your bills for two or three months, you could have your electricity, gas, telephone, and other utilities cut off. You could get hit with interest or late fees. Plus, failing to pay your bills is a fast way to wreck your credit history.

If you don't think you'll be able to cope with basic personal finance in a time of crisis, you need to set up a system ahead of time to make sure your checks get deposited and your bills get paid. The Internet and electronic banking can be extremely useful in this situation.

If you opt to have your check deposited electronically into your money market or checking account, you won't have to worry about physically going to the bank and depositing the money. And, the cash will actually get into your account faster, which means you have control over the funds more quickly than if you had to wait for your check to clear. Ask your employer if the company payroll system is set up for electronic deposits. I'm guessing that if you work for even a small company, this option will be available for you.

Next, you need to see what kind of automatic billing you can put into place. Most of the telephone, cell phone, Internet, cable, satellite, and newspaper companies will allow you to pay for their services with a credit card. If that's the case, they can probably set you up to pay automatically by credit card each month. That means you won't have to write a separate check for each of these products and services. Some insurance companies will allow you to give them a credit card number and they will automatically bill you for your annual premiums. (But don't pay extra just for the convenience.)

If you can cut down the monthly checks you write from twenty or thirty to four or five, it's less likely that you'll wind up paying bills late. And you'll save on the postage, which for thirty bills per month costs you an additional eleven dollars.

This method assumes that you are responsible enough to pay your credit card bill in full at the end of each month. If you can't, you'll end up paying interest needlessly on all of these charges. If you're swamped with credit card debt before a crisis hits, you may find yourself sinking further and further into the hole. That's also why it's important to stay on top of your bills when a crisis happens.

Each month, I write just a handful of checks: usually two checks to pay off each credit card bill (in full!), and a couple of other checks to different places, depending on the month. Not only will this same system simplify your life in the event of a crisis, it will reduce your bill-paying sessions to just a few minutes per month.

A GOOD START

Take out your checkbook and look at the different checks you write over the course of a month. If you're like most people, you'll write regular checks to companies that provide the following services:

- Rent (apartment, office, studio, or parking space)
- Internet access or web hosting
- Credit card companies
- Telephone
- Cell phone, pager, or wireless Internet service
- Cable or satellite
- Electricity, water, gas, garbage pickup, or other utilities
- Mortgage, and perhaps an extra amount for real estate taxes and insurance premiums
- Insurance-related items, such as premiums or deductibles
- Auto or school loan payments
- Tuition and other educational expenses
- Newspaper or magazine delivery
- Day care or babysitter
- Health insurance premiums or co-pays
- Health club or other club dues

For those companies you pay regularly, call and ask if they can bill your credit card instead. Typically, companies are happy to do this, as they receive their cash much more quickly and don't have to worry about checks that bounce.

If the first person in customer service or billing can't help you, ask to speak to a supervisor. This is particularly true with telephone companies. I have had all kinds of problems through the years getting through to someone at various telephone companies who knows how to set up a pay-by-charge-card account. Once it's in place, it works beautifully. But the setup can be annoying.

Finally, if you use Quicken or Microsoft Money, many credit card companies (including Discover) have software on their Web sites that will allow you to download your charges directly into your financial software. The benefit, of course, is that your expenditures are seamlessly recorded with little extra work for you.

Small Business Owners

Billing regular expenses to a company credit card can help simplify your record-keeping, including telephone, Internet access, web hosting, insurance premiums, and utilities. And if you use QuickBooks, you or your bookkeeper can download the charges from the company credit card directly into your software. Since you can print out a list of your credit card charges each month, it's easy to compare expenditures on a month-to-month basis.

SIMPLE STEP
12

TAKE ADVANTAGE OF E-BANKING

In the mid-1990s my former bank started offering customers the opportunity to bank online. They touted the move as a way for consumers to have more control over their cash. But since banks rarely offer things that are better for the consumer without also being better (sometimes outstandingly so) for the bank, I was a bit suspicious.

Sure enough, the bank wanted to charge scads of money for the privilege of allowing you to manage more of your own accounts, do your own transfers and check-writing, and basically save the bank loads of cash.

Back then, the electronic finance and online worlds were very young, and there were concerns about firewalls and privacy, and everyone wondered if a hacker could tap into your account and basically liquidate it without your knowledge.

There are still the same concerns, and others. Someone might steal your identity, open up a charge account, and quickly leave you $20,000 in debt. However, even if a hacker could liquidate your account, there would be records to help get that account back to where it was prior to the attack. And having access to those records, not to mention having your accounts online and available 24/7/365, is an excellent reason to use e-banking in order to help protect your finances in a crisis.

Having electronic or online accounts means you're not

tied to your paper statements. Sure, you can always get backup copies of your statements from your bank. And you can even get copies of your cancelled checks (though some banks charge for this). But by paying your bills electronically, you always have the ability to pay your bills on time, no matter what happens to the paper records of the account or your checkbook.

Not only that, but depending on what your e-banking service charges, you'll be able to save some money. Why? Because the cash will stay in your account longer (earning any interest your account bears), and you won't be paying postage.

Today, it doesn't matter if your bank doesn't offer its own brand-name electronic banking option. Portals including Yahoo!, Bills.com, Excite, Go2Net, MSN, Quicken, CheckFree, and even the United States Post Office offer you the ability to pay your bills electronically no matter which bank is yours.

E-Trade Accounts

Most major investment firms, such as Charles Schwab, Fidelity Investments, Vanguard, Merrill Lynch, and others, plus Internet-only firms like Ameritrade, offer fast Web sites chock-full of useful information available only to clients. Best of all, when you do buy or sell stocks and mutual funds, the cost of the trades is nominal, usually less than $25.

In terms of managing your cash in a crisis, trading online is another way to untie you from the paper statements that you receive each month. If you trade online, you can go to the Web site of your investment firm at any time of the day or night and see what your accounts are worth. You can take advantage of pie charts, calculators, and information from analysts that can help you make a decision about buying, selling, or holding a company's stock. You can even print out a copy of your holdings and net worth at any given moment, making it much more accurate than your month-end statement. And you can do it from any computer or hand-held device that is linked to the Internet.

A GOOD START

CheckFree.com is the site that appears to power many of the other online bill-paying systems. CheckFree works with Yahoo!, Bills.com, Excite, Go2Net, and many other bill-paying systems.

But prices vary. The current deal (as this book went to press) for consumers offers you three months of electronic bill-paying service for free. After that the fees vary by a few bucks. At Yahoo!, you will spend $4.95 per month for twelve payments, plus forty cents for each additional e-check you send. At Bills.com, you'll pay $7.00 per month, but that entitles you to pay twenty bills, plus forty cents for each additional e-check you write. The U.S. Post Office charges $6.95 for twenty checks, plus fifty cents for each additional check you write.

The fees for small business owners are slightly higher, probably because there are fewer companies offering the service. You'll pay $18.95 for thirty checks and fifty cents for each additional check. And your company will typically only get one month free.

There are over three hundred companies that can send you your bill electronically, including all of the major credit cards and the *Wall Street Journal*. You can instruct the e-pay systems to pay your bills regularly, so instead of you directing when the payments are sent, the system can be set up to pay all of your electronic bills by the due date, freeing you from worrying about it at all.

Also, many of these systems are set up to work with either Quicken, QuickBooks, or Microsoft Money financial management software, which should simplify record-keeping. One caveat: Typically, these e-pay systems require four business days to process your check. If you go to DiscoverCard.com and pay your bill there directly, the cash is instantly withdrawn from your account and the bill is paid. So remember to give yourself a few extra days. At least it's faster than snail mail. (You may want to record your e-pay confirmation numbers in your palm pilot for easy access.)

If You're Not Ready to Jump In

Another way to pay your bills electronically is to load all of your monthly bills—or as many as you can—onto your credit card. Then log on to your credit card company's Web site and pay your bill directly. Discover Card and American Express are two examples. They permit you to log on, fill out a form with the information on your check, and then send an electronic check to pay your bill online. You don't have to pay your bill this way every month (although I do), but it's a good backup system to have to make sure your bills get paid.

Small Business Owners

Whether you have one employee or 150, you may want to invest in an electronic payroll system, in addition to paying your bills electronically. Because companies like Sure-Payroll.com and Quicken keep track of all of your employees' payment information, as well as tax and retirement fund contributions, you don't have to worry about losing important payroll data, or being late with your employees' paychecks in the event of a crisis. And should the unthinkable happen, your records are safeguarded and available to you 24/7/365.

SIMPLE STEP
13

KEEP SOME CREDIT
IN YOUR OWN NAME

When my friend Pam lost her husband, one of the first things that happened was that her credit card company immediately cancelled their joint credit card. They reenrolled her into her own credit card, but slashed the credit limit. Clearly, this had an effect on her credit history, not to mention the types of offers that used to come in the mail: no more offers to test-drive $100,000 Mercedes. Certain catalogues stopped coming, as did special offers from other credit card companies.

What Pam didn't realize is that she could have called her credit card company and demanded that it continue the same account under the same credit limit. Husbands and wives share credit, even if one spouse earns the money and the other one stays home.

But because your credit score (a number derived from assigning a numerical value to different parts of your credit history) places weight on the length of time you've had different credit cards, Pam was dinged because the account she and her husband had shared for years was closed and a new line of credit was opened. That sort of thing can significantly, and negatively, affect your credit score—which directly affects the types of credit card deals and mortgage rates you're offered.

That's why it's always a good idea to keep one credit card account in your own name. No matter what happens to your joint credit, having a single account for a long period of time will help stabilize your credit score. In a time of emergency, such as a job loss, having good credit and a high credit score may allow you to get a quick home equity loan. Many lenders will allow you to borrow up to $20,000 or even $30,000 without verifying your income (important when you lose a job). That ready access to cash could help out in a crisis.

A GOOD START

Try to keep one credit card account in your own name, without using your spouse or a friend to qualify. Make sure you keep the account active, and use it at least a couple of times a year. Since this card will probably be your reserve card, choose one that doesn't charge an annual fee. And make sure you pay it off completely at the end of each month.

The longer you have the same credit cards, the better off your credit score will be.

— 3 —

Travel

SIMPLE STEP

14

BUY AIRLINE TICKETS AND RENT CARS WITH A CREDIT CARD THAT OFFERS FREE LIFE INSURANCE

Whenever I buy an airline ticket, I'm careful to charge it to one of my credit cards that offers free life insurance. For example, Discover Card offers a free $500,000 life insurance benefit should something happen during the flight. If my plane crashes and I die, my heirs will have an extra $500,000 in life insurance that they otherwise wouldn't have had.

Best of all, it doesn't cost me anything. It is a benefit that comes with using a Discover Card.

Many cards provide different benefits. Some offer additional insurance when renting a car. For example, if I charge a rental car with my Visa, it will provide supplemental insurance over and above what my own car insurance policy provides. I won't get to make a claim from both policies, but in case of an accident, I should be covered without having to fork over big bucks for the car rental agency's policy.

A GOOD START

It's important to read the fine print before you rely on any insurance policy. Make sure you understand the benefits being offered and what they will and will not cover. For example, the free car insurance may not work if I rent a car in a foreign country, or if I somehow violate the terms and conditions of the policy.

If you don't understand exactly what the policy covers, you can check out your credit card company's Web site, or call their toll-free customer service number and have the entire policy sent to you.

Years ago, Sam and I went to Mexico to visit some friends. We rented a white Volkswagen Beetle and drove to Cuernavaca. As we were pulling out of a mall, all of a sudden, we heard a CRUNCH! and felt something riding onto our car.

We turned around to see a huge Chevy Suburban that the driver had driven up onto the rear end of our car! His car was so enormous, he hadn't even seen us.

If you get into a car accident in the United States and no one is hurt, you might exchange insurance information with the other driver and then either drive to the nearest police station (to file an accident report) or go home. In Mexico, you stand by your car and wait until the insurance adjusters show up, negotiate fault and expenses, sign papers, and allow you to go. (This process could take several hours.)

Sam and I were so thankful that we had chosen to buy full insurance coverage from the car rental agency when we rented the car. We had called ahead and found out that our credit card didn't cover accident insurance for international car rentals. Although our own automobile policy might have covered it, an accident would have caused a blemish on our record. So we bought coverage at the rental office. Although it cost us another twenty dollars a day for the insurance premiums, it was terrific to know that no matter what happened, we would be covered.

SHARE YOUR TRAVEL ITINERARY
WITH YOUR FRIENDS AND FAMILY

My mother recently took a trip to Cuba. As it happened, she left for the island just two days after Hurricane Michelle had rammed its way through, destroying some 45,000 homes and most of the island's sugarcane crop. With 130-mile-per-hour winds, the storm was the fiercest in over half a century.

But what if my mother had been on the island during the hurricane? Or what if something happened here and we needed to reach her? My mother always lets us know where she's going when she travels. She provides us with her dates of departure and arrival, the flight information, hotels with telephone and fax numbers, and other information that would prove useful in an emergency. (In fact, she encourages us to fax her while she's away with all the news from home so she doesn't feel like she's missing anything!)

If someone (at least one person) doesn't know how to reach you in times of crisis, you may miss an opportunity to make a decision that could profoundly affect your financial future.

If you're the kind of person who likes to "disappear" for days, weeks, or months at a time, you could find yourself not being a part of family decisions. You may receive family news and information later because no one could reach you. You may miss a court date because your attorney didn't know where to find you. Conversely, if you run into trouble, your paper trail will help your loved ones get to you faster.

When Sherri decided to spend her fortieth year traveling around the world, she investigated ways in which friends and family members could send her mail to the different countries she had decided to visit. She also looked for places where she could check her e-mail account. Because she planned which countries she would travel to in advance (and approximately when she'd be there), she was able to get addresses for local post offices and American Express offices for friends and family.

A frequent traveler who picks up and goes for days or weeks at a time, Jonathan came up with an inventive solution to let his friends and family know where he'd be traveling—he built a Web site and used his laptop to update the site as to his travel plans. He also posted digital photos and travelogs of the esoteric places he'd visited. Friends and family members could e-mail him no matter where he traveled. Because he checked his e-mail frequently, he could get urgent messages and respond to them.

A GOOD START

When you travel, you should send a written itinerary—nothing fancy, just the facts will do nicely—to your family. If you're taking an extensive trip, or if you're planning to live abroad for several weeks or months, make sure you provide all of the contact information to at least one friend or family member.

If you travel frequently, you may wish to invest in a cell phone that works all over the country, or abroad, or invest in a worldwide paging system. Also, consider starting up an e-mail account that you can access from any computer worldwide (Yahoo! offers free e-mail and is easily accessed worldwide). By giving your loved ones a way to contact you during your travels, you decrease the odds that something unfortunate will happen that will affect your financial future.

SIMPLE STEP
16

CONSIDER BUYING
TRAVEL INSURANCE

If you're scheduled to fly for a family vacation across the country, you've probably invested at least $200 per person per ticket, plus you might have had to put down a nonrefundable deposit on a portion of your trip. If you're scheduled to take a cruise, you might have had to pay for the entire trip up front.

So what happens if someone dies, loses their job, is hospitalized, or suffers some other catastrophe? What if there is a hurricane on your island, or you fall down and break your leg on the first day of your holiday? You'd probably lose all of the money you had put down on the trip. That might be okay if you've spent just $250 on a ticket home to see your parents. But it might be too much money to lose if you've spent $3,000 on a dream vacation.

There are different sorts of travel insurance policies that can cover you, from accidental death, to trip cancellations, lost or delayed luggage, or medical emergencies. Typically, travel insurance covers losses caused by trip cancellation or interruption. You're reimbursed for nonrefundable payments if you have to cancel your trip because of:

- Sudden illness or death of a family member or traveling companion

- Bad weather (like a hurricane or earthquake)

- Jury duty

- Flood or fire in your home

- Civil action, war, or terrorist activity in the area in which you're going (though in the wake of the September 11 terrorist attacks, some insurers are now thinking about charging separately for terrorist insurance, if they'll provide it at all)

- Bankruptcy of an airline, cruise line, or tour operator

Typically, you'll be covered for nonrefundable expenses, baggage delay, or loss up to $1,000, plus another $200 or so per person to buy "necessities" if your bags are delayed more than twelve to twenty-four hours. (Be aware that there are limits and exclusions to the coverage, including laptop computers and other electronic gear, jewelry, and cameras.)

The way this really works, of course, is that you will probably have to shell out all of the money and wait to be reimbursed by the airline several weeks (or months) later. If your bag turns up a week later, the airlines might not reimburse you at all; or, you'll really have to fight for it. You can prepare for the worst by hand-carrying all of your most important valuables plus your cosmetics and a change of clothes onto the airplane. Although the amount you're able to carry on has been limited to one carry-on plus a personal item, you may wish to just bring what you can carry on rather than risk losing something and adding aggravation to your trip.

Your Own Insurance

Your existing homeowner's, auto, and health policies may cover some of your financial loss if, for example, you get into a car accident (provided your policy covers you when renting a car) or if your camera is stolen. But check to make sure your health insurance policy will cover you for medical treatment abroad (many don't, or will charge you a supplemental cost for the coverage). If you have Medicare, it basically will not cover you for medical treatment received abroad, so you will need to purchase insurance to cover this gap.

If you're taking an adventure travel trip, you will probably need to purchase additional insurance coverage, since many U.S. health insurers exclude skydiving, bungee jumping, hang gliding, mountain climbing, or scuba diving when abroad.

A GOOD START

You can buy insurance until you're broke. Or spend more than you're paying for the trip itself. How much should you spend on travel insurance?

- Flight insurance (if you don't get it for free when you buy your ticket) should cost you around ten dollars per flight.

- Travel cancellation policies should cost 4 percent of the price of your trip.

- Medical policies should cost $50 to $1,000, depending on the coverage needed.

- Package travel insurance, which bundles together individual coverage, should run between 4.5 and 6.5 percent of your cost.

- Discounts are available to seniors or for two family members traveling together.

Talk to your travel agent about the level of travel insurance he or she offers (yes, he or she will probably earn a commission from selling it to you). Ask the agent to fax or e-mail all of the details of the policy. Read it before you agree to pay for it. You might also price out policies at insurance and travel Web sites, including InsureMyTrip.com, Expedia.com, Orbitz.com, and Travelocity.com.

Finally, whether you should buy insurance comes down to two factors: How much will you have to pay for the coverage you need, and can you live with the financial loss? Weigh these two side by side before you commit to your travel insurance policy.

Years ago, when I lived in Britain, I knew some university students who would buy trip insurance anytime they would travel abroad. Because they were students, they could buy a pretty good policy for just a few dollars. The first few trips, I couldn't believe they were so careless—or had such bad luck. Something bad always happened and a new camera, tape recorder, video camera, or clothing always disappeared. I later learned that it was a bit of a scam. These students always filed a claim as a way to make a few bucks off the "establishment."

If something does happen and you have a loss, you'll probably need to provide a police report to the insurance company as proof. Be sure to read the policy to find out what kind of proof is required ahead of time. It would be much more difficult to contact a police station in a tiny Italian village once you're back at home in Kansas.

4

Insurance and Health

GET REGULAR CHECKUPS

Big problems often start out as little problems that get ignored during the hustle and bustle of our daily lives. A small toothache, for example, might turn into a very expensive root canal by the time we make time to see the dentist two years later, especially since few health plans include any reimbursement for dental work.

That's why getting regular checkups is an important part of life. Seeing the dentist twice a year (or three times, if you have a history of dental problems), may seem expensive in the short run, but getting good dental care can save you thousands of dollars later on in life.

The same is true for other kinds of medical doctors. Women should see a gynecologist once a year to have the basic battery of tests, including a pap smear. Women over forty should consider a mammogram every year to increase the odds of catching and treating breast cancer while it is still in its early stages, or follow their doctor's recommendations. Men should have regular prostate exams once they're forty, as part of regular physical exams. Ask your doctor when you'll need a colonoscopy to screen for colon cancer, which is highly curable if detected early, and how often you'll need a blood cholesterol check to detect coronary heart disease.

From a financial point of view, it's far less expensive to pay for "well care," as it's come to be known—even if it's out of your pocket—than it is to pay for something that's become much more serious. Before scheduling any appointments, check with your insurance company to see if such preventive care is covered and whether you need preauthorization. Once you or a family member has been diagnosed with a serious disease, buying various forms of insurance, from health to life to long-term care disability, is either very expensive or even impossible.

So take care of yourself today. If you can prevent—or just push off by a few years—a serious illness by making sure your body is in as good a shape as possible, the financial benefits will be the least of those you enjoy. You'll also enjoy feeling better and being able to do more with your life. But perhaps the best benefit of good health is that it will help you better weather the stress of a disaster.

A GOOD START

Bad habits are not only expensive, but they can cause some of the more serious diseases. For example, if you smoke, stop. In addition to the numerous health-related benefits, you'll likely be able to lower the cost for your life, health, automobile, and even long-term care insurance policies.

Skydiving, bungee jumping, and other high-risk sports give some people a huge adrenaline rush. But in addition to being extremely expensive, participating in high-risk sports can make it impossible for you to buy the insurance protection you need. For example, skydivers generally cannot buy life insurance. If you're married, with children, consider giving up these sports so you can buy the financial protection your family will need in a crisis.

Finally, if you haven't seen your doctors recently, make a list and start making your appointments. You should have your eyes checked for glaucoma every few years when you're young, and then annually as you reach middle age. Visit the dentist at least twice a year. See your general physician once a year or every eighteen months for a complete physical. Women should have a pap smear once a year and a mammogram as the doctor recommends once you reach the age of forty.

SIMPLE STEP

18

EVALUATE YOUR CURRENT
INSURANCE POLICIES

Do you have enough insurance to protect yourself and your family in the event of a disaster?

That's the million-dollar question these days. Insurance exists to protect us financially from the effects of an unexpected loss, whether a car, a home, a business, or a spouse or partner. Evaluating whether the insurance you've purchased will provide the protection you need is the next issue you need to tackle.

The basic forms of insurance include:

Homeowner's or Renter's Insurance: Protects you in case something happens to your home, or its contents.

Automobile Insurance: Protects you if there is damage to your vehicle or damage to property or to someone else caused by your vehicle. It also protects you from lawsuits and judgments.

Umbrella Insurance: Covers you for catastrophic loss or damage above and beyond the liability limits of your other policies.

Long-Term Care Insurance: Pays for all, or most of, a stay in a nursing home or long-term care facility, typically up to five years.

Disability Insurance: Replaces up to 70 percent of your income if you're sidelined due to a long-term disability.

Flood Insurance: Backed by the U.S. government, flood insurance will reimburse you up to $250,000 for damage caused to your home due to a flood, if you live in a flood plain. General flood insurance may be available at a higher price if you live outside of a federally designated flood plain or if the value of your home and its contents exceeds $250,000.

Earthquake Insurance: Available in limited areas around the country, and generally necessary only if you live on or near a fault line.

Health Insurance: Provides you with coverage for all medical-related emergencies.

Life Insurance: Pays the beneficiary cash if the policy-holder dies.

Business Insurance: Covers your losses in case of business interruption, theft, loss of office and its contents, and other issues.

In evaluating your policies, you'll want to look at how much it will cost you to replace whatever gets destroyed. Then, check how much coverage you have. Ideally, your coverage will cover most, if not all, of the replacement cost of whatever it is you've lost.

For example, let's say your business is destroyed by fire. It's a total loss. While you probably don't have to pay rent, you are losing business each day. On top of that, you have to find another space to rent, furnish the new space, order new business cards and stationery, new phone systems, computers, and dozens of other kinds of expensive equipment. If you have the proper business insurance, you should receive a check from your insurance company that will cover most, if not all, of these expenses.

If a tree falls down and smashes your garage, which just happens to have your new car inside of it, your home-owner's insurance will reimburse you for the cost of rebuilding your garage. Your automobile insurance will pay to replace your car.

But if you haven't kept your business or homeowner's insurance up to date, or if you don't have adequate cover-age, there's a very real chance that you may be out a very large amount of cash. That's a financially precarious posi-tion in which to find yourself. Make sure it doesn't happen to you.

A GOOD START

You can go broke buying insurance policies. On the other hand, if you don't have enough protection, you could go broke replacing what you've lost. How do you know if you have enough protection? Start by making a list of the poli-cies you currently hold and how much they will pay in the worst-case situation:

Insurance Worksheet

Type of Insurance	Annual Cost	Amount of Coverage
Homeowner's/renter's	_____	_____
Automobile	_____	_____
Umbrella	_____	_____
Long-term care	_____	_____
Disability	_____	_____
Flood	_____	_____
Earthquake	_____	_____
Health	_____	_____
Life	_____	_____

Next, think about how much it will cost you to replace what you've lost. For example, if you have to replace $50,000 a year in annual salary, you may need a million-dollar life insurance policy that earns 5 percent. If your car is only worth $1,500, and you're a good driver, perhaps you need to pay only for third-party collision insurance, which means that you insure anyone you hit but not damage to your own vehicle.

Finally, match the amount of each coverage you have with your potential losses in a worst-case situation. Does your homeowner's or renter's coverage have guaranteed replacement coverage? In other words, do you get enough cash to replace the item at today's prices, or do you just get what you paid for that couch twenty years ago? Can you find a decent, used $1,500 car to replace the one that got totaled, or will you need to shell out more?

By comparing numbers and reading the fine print on your policies, you'll begin to have a better understanding of where your coverage works and where it falls short.

In the next few Simple Steps, I'll take an in-depth look at different forms of insurance and how to better evaluate whether you've got a good policy for the right price.

INVENTORY YOUR PERSONAL AND BUSINESS ASSETS

It's difficult to determine whether you have enough insurance until you know what you have and how much it's worth. By taking an inventory of your personal and business assets, you'll create a lasting record of what you own, which can then be assessed for its worth and updated as necessary.

In Your House

Start going through your home room by room. Create a worksheet for each room, writing down what you have, the year in which it was purchased, and the cost to replace the item if you had to purchase it today. I've included a sample worksheet at the end of this Step.

What should you include in your master list? Everything. This is a time to be as detailed as possible. For example, in your living room you might have a couch, two chairs, two end tables, a coffee table, an area rug, curtains or other window treatments, assorted electronic equipment, a piano, twelve paintings, two framed posters, and several vases, bowls, photos in frames, and so on. You might have a bookshelf that is filled with books, photo albums, knickknacks, and other items.

Be sure to itemize all of your furniture, clothing, shoes, jewelry and watches, decorations and furnishings, bedding, light fixtures, computers, rugs and carpets. In the kitchen, be sure to include your pots, pans, dishes, large and small appliances, light fixtures, cookbooks, and anything else you'd have to replace. Don't forget any collections: china, silver, baseball cards, stamps, or coins. Be sure to visit the garage (lawn furniture, tools, mowers, sporting equipment, etc.) and list items stored in your basement and attic. If you store items in a storage locker, be sure to inventory the contents there as well.

A Picture Is Worth 1,000 Words

It's important to write everything down, but it's an even better idea to back up what you've written with a photographic record. You can either videotape or photograph (with a digital or conventional camera) the contents of your home and office (or do both to be really secure). You will want to take a picture of everything you've written down on your list, in order to prove that you have the item. If your video or camera has a time/date stamp, figure out how to use it. In case disaster does strike, you'll want to be able to prove that you owned these items.

I suggest you consider buying an inexpensive digital camera or borrow a friend's. Digital photos can be stored on a CD (using your CD-rewrite drive), online at a portal like Yahoo!, or online at your own Web site. The benefit to storing your photos electronically, online, is that they can be easily downloaded and viewed—as long as you provide the site address and password. Or, consider burning your own CDs, which you'll store in a safe place.

If something does happen, the insurance adjuster who is assigned to your case will have ample evidence to support your inventory of items missing. In order to keep your photographic record safe, keep a copy in your home safe and another copy in your safe deposit box.

Small Business Owners

Many small business owners lost everything in the World Trade Center terrorist attacks. While many insurance companies quickly reimbursed business owners up to their insurance policy maximums and didn't ask a whole lot of questions, you might have to fight hard for every nickel you get when disaster strikes your business.

Keeping a photographic record of your office equipment, furniture and furnishings, artwork, and any other valuables in the office space will only help your insurance adjuster determine a fair settlement more quickly.

A GOOD START

Here's a worksheet to help you start to inventory your home and/or small business's contents.

Inventory the Contents of Your Home or Office Worksheet

Living Room	Date Bought	Estimated Replacement Cost
Couch		
Loveseat		
Chair(s)		
Side table(s)		
Coffee table(s)		
Fireplace equipment		
Curtains/window treatments		
Rug/area rug		
Light fixture(s)		
Flooring		
Armoire(s)/bookcases		
Television		
Stereo equipment		
Other electronic equipment		
CDs/albums/tapes		
Artwork*		
Books		
Collectibles		

Kitchen	Date Purchased	Replacement Cost
Stove		
Refrigerator		
Oven(s)		
Hood		
Microwave		
Dishwasher		
Sink/faucets		
Washer/dryer		
Cabinets		

*Most insurance policies limit the replacement value of artwork, jewelry, and fur coats, unless you have had the item specifically appraised.

Kitchen *(cont'd)*	**Date Purchased**	**Replacement Cost**
Light fixture(s)	_____	_____
Floor	_____	_____
Dishes	_____	_____
Glassware	_____	_____
Silverware	_____	_____
Pots and pans	_____	_____
Artwork	_____	_____
Vases	_____	_____
Pottery	_____	_____
Tablecloths	_____	_____
Sterling silver/silverplate	_____	_____
Candlesticks	_____	_____
Food	_____	_____
Wine/alcohol	_____	_____
Miscellaneous	_____	_____

Den/Family Room	**Date Purchased**	**Replacement Cost**
Chairs	_____	_____
Couches	_____	_____
Bookshelves	_____	_____
Books	_____	_____
TV	_____	_____
Stereo	_____	_____
Computer/other electronics	_____	_____
Rug/flooring/carpet	_____	_____
Light fixtures	_____	_____
Tables	_____	_____
Curtains/window treatments	_____	_____
Artwork	_____	_____
Vases	_____	_____
Photo albums	_____	_____
Plants	_____	_____
Knickknacks	_____	_____
Miscellaneous	_____	_____

Dining Room	**Date Purchased**	**Replacement Cost**
Table		
Chairs		
Light fixture(s)		
Display case		
Bookcase		
Sideboard		
Rug/carpet		
Window treatments		

Bedroom	**Date Purchased**	**Replacement Cost**
Bed(s)/crib		
Night table(s)		
Light fixture(s)		
Chair(s)		
Couch(es)		
Television		
VCR/DVD		
Computers/other electronics		
Rug/flooring/carpet		
Sheets, blankets		
Clothes		
Shoes		
Bookshelves		
Books		
Jewelry/watches		
Miscellaneous		

Garage	**Date Purchased**	**Replacement Cost**
Car 1		
Car 2		
Car 3		
Lawn mower		
Snow blower		
Leaf blower		

Garage *(cont'd)*	**Date Purchased**	**Replacement Cost**
Barbeque	_____	_____
Assorted tools	_____	_____
Beach chairs	_____	_____
Lawn furniture	_____	_____
Ladders	_____	_____
Sporting equipment	_____	_____
Miscellaneous	_____	_____

Bathroom	**Date Purchased**	**Replacement Cost**
Vanity	_____	_____
Tub/Jacuzzi	_____	_____
Scale	_____	_____
Toilet	_____	_____
Toiletries	_____	_____
Towels	_____	_____
Hamper	_____	_____

Home Office	**Date Purchased**	**Replacement Cost**
Desk(s)	_____	_____
Chair(s)	_____	_____
Table(s)	_____	_____
Couch(es)	_____	_____
Computer(s)	_____	_____
Printer(s)	_____	_____
Scanner(s)	_____	_____
Telephone(s)	_____	_____
Hand-held device(s)	_____	_____
Light fixture(s)	_____	_____
Filing cabinet(s)	_____	_____
Bookshelves	_____	_____
Supplies	_____	_____
Records	_____	_____
Inventory	_____	_____
Bulletin board(s)	_____	_____
Artwork	_____	_____

Home Office *(cont'd)*   **Date Purchased**   **Replacement Cost**
Plants   _____   _____
Shredder   _____   _____

Stored items   **Date Purchased**   **Replacement Cost**

_____   _____   _____
_____   _____   _____
_____   _____   _____

Basements and Attics

Don't forget to do an inventory of everything in your basement and in your attic. If you haven't been down to your basement in a while, or if you have boxes still waiting to be unpacked from your move (no matter how long ago that was), check out the contents and include them in your inventory.

Finally, if you don't know how to gauge the replacement value of a particular item, call your insurance agent for guidance, or read your policy. Add it all up. Does your homeowner's insurance cover it all? If not, time to update your policy. Check out the next Simple Step for details.

UPDATE YOUR HOMEOWNER'S
OR RENTER'S POLICY

I lived at home for a year after I graduated from college. I was earning very little money and my grandfather thought I should try and save something before moving out. After a year, a friend and I rented a two-bedroom apartment not far from where my family lived.

About five months into the lease I came home to find the door double-locked from the inside (we didn't have that key). Knowing my roommate was out of town, I started pounding on the door, yelling and screaming. I heard a scuffle inside and some glass breaking. I ran down to the neighbors, who let me in, and went up the back stairs. I discovered my kitchen window had been broken and someone had robbed our apartment. Because I started pounding on the door during the middle of the robbery, I apparently cut their activities short. They got a color television, a cheap boom box, and some of my roommate's gold jewelry. Because my room was at the front of the house, the only thing of mine they had time to take was an opal necklace my great aunt Ruth had given me.

I think often about that necklace and that robbery. The cops thought it was a couple of neighborhood kids looking for some easy money. I was glad not to have been hurt. But the loss of that necklace stung.

When the police were filling out the report, they asked me if I had renter's insurance. I was twenty-two and I had never heard of it.

Renter's insurance protects the contents of your home in case of loss due to theft, fire, and many other hazards. Homeowner's insurance protects the contents of your home, but it also protects you from the loss of, or damage to, the home itself (something you don't need if you rent because the landlord owns the property).

No one is going to make you purchase renter's insurance. It's completely optional. (Of course, the day after my robbery, I bought a $20,000 policy and found out how inexpensive it really is.) But if you buy a home with a mortgage, the lender will require you to buy enough homeowner's insurance (also called hazard insurance in some parts of the country) to cover at least the amount of the loan. (Since you've pledged the house as collateral for the loan, they want to know they're protected in case something happens.) If you're wise, you'll cover not just the loan, but the total cost of rebuilding the home, should it be completely destroyed, and replacing your possessions.

If you don't have homeowner's or renter's insurance, your losses could be substantial. Let's say you're living in a house with an attached garage. And let's say a hundred-year-old tree on the property falls and crashes into the garage, destroying the garage and your brand-new car. If you're a renter, you don't have liability for the property (unless you cut down the tree for some reason). Your car insurance might cover the value of the car, but you'd be out of luck for anything else you've stored in the garage. If you're the homeowner, you'll not only lose the contents of the garage but be out of pocket to repair or replace the garage itself.

Homeowner's Insurance Perils

According to the Insurance Information Institute (www.iii
.org), a nonprofit information group for the property/
casualty insurance industry, your homeowner's policy
should cover the perils or calamities contained in the following list:

- Fire or lightning
- Windstorm or hail
- An explosion
- An aircraft or car ramming through the wall or ceiling
  of the home, damaging walkways, lawns, a pool, or
  other features of the property
- Smoke
- Vandalism and malicious mischief
- Theft
- Breakage of glass constituting part of the building,
  such as windows or skylights
- Falling objects; damage from weight of snow, sleet, or
  ice; collapse of building(s)
- Sudden and accidental tearing apart, cracking, burn-
  ing, or bulging of a steam or hot water heating system
  or of appliances for heating water
- Freezing of plumbing, heating, or air-conditioning
  systems and/or household appliances
- Sudden and accidental damage from artificially generated currents to electrical appliances, devices, fixtures,
  and wiring (TV and radio tubes are not included, if you
  happen to have either lying around)

What Isn't Covered

Floods, earthquakes, and mudslides are never covered by a regular homeowner's policy. A "riot of civil commotion" generally isn't covered either, so if your home team wins the basketball game and there's looting after the game and your house is damaged or destroyed, you may be out of luck. But you can buy separate coverage for each of these things, which I'll talk about in the following Steps.

Other types of perils for which there may be no coverage on a general policy include damage caused by land disturbances, chemical or paint spills, backed-up sewers and drains (you may get this if you have a sump pump), wild beasts, and scorching without fire.

You should also ask your agent if your living expenses will be covered while you're fixing or rebuilding your home. Be sure to read the fine print.

Damage from Terrorist Activities

Since September 11, 2001, acts of terrorism (which have previously been covered under almost all residential policies) may or may not be included when your policy comes up for renewal. Insurance companies, reeling from the financial loss on that date, reassessed commercial and business policies with regard to acts of terrorism, and dramatically increased the cost of those policies. Warren Buffett, whose Berkshire Hathaway owns one of the largest insurance companies in the world, in assessing the financial cost of September 11, said his company and the entire insurance industry had been giving away terrorist coverage for free and would no longer do so. So if you have a small business, expect to pay more for additional coverage that protects you from the loss of property due to terrorism. I'm guessing that over the next few years damage from terrorist activities will be excluded from many homeowner's insurance policies, but coverage will be available for a separate fee.

Guaranteed Replacement Cost

When comparing policies, you'll want to look at the deductible, the property and possessions coverage, and what type of coverage you're buying. The best type of home-owner's insurance coverage is called *guaranteed replacement cost*. That means the insurance company will pay to rebuild your home no matter what the cost, even if it exceeds the total cost of your policy (on some policies, there is usually a limit of 120 to 125 percent of your policy). There is typically an inflation rider built into the policy to make sure the total value of the policy increases each year.

Replacement insurance guarantees only that the insurer will rebuild your home as it stands today, not taking any building code changes into account, or even if you can rebuild your same home on your lot due to zoning changes. And if the rebuilding costs more than the total value of your policy, you're out of luck. A *cash-value* policy will reimburse you based only on your property's current market value, not what it would cost to build new.

In many parts of the country, true guaranteed cost replacement insurance is no longer available. You'll have to ask your agent what is and isn't covered, and if there are exclusions. Your insurance company might estimate that replacing your home will cost only $60 per square foot. Realistically, the cost might be $150 or higher.

Homeowner's insurance policies typically limit the contents coverage for your home to half of the total policy limit. So if your home is insured for $500,000, your contents coverage will likely be limited to $250,000 plus any special riders for fur coats, jewelry, and artwork. Ask if the contents coverage is guaranteed replacement as well. And pay attention to the cost-per-square-foot calculations.

How much is enough? You won't know until you take an inventory of your home and assess how much it will cost to replace each item at current prices.

Martha and Jaime lived in a beautiful Victorian home for many years. They had, over the years, restored much of the home's detail themselves, including scraping and sanding beautiful oak woodwork, replastering many walls, and replacing knob-and-tube wiring with conduit.

One winter night, their Christmas tree ignited. The house burst into flames, and most of it was destroyed. Martha and Jaime were able to escape with a few mementos.

The house had to be torn down. When they met the insurance adjuster at the site a few days later, he agreed to pay them the maximum under their policy. But when Martha and Jaime received the check, they were flabbergasted to find out that it was only for $250,000, plus another $125,000 for their contents.

Their home would ultimately cost them more than $400,000 to rebuild (but of course you can't rebuild 100-year-old wood moldings) and another $100,000 to furnish. The extra $100,000 came out of their own pockets.

The problem was that Martha and Jaime never updated the policy to reflect the increased cost to rebuild their home. The $250,000 cost was what they originally paid for the home years earlier.

Small Business Owners

If you have a home office, you may need a special rider to your homeowner's policy that covers the office equipment and furniture in your home office. Check with your agent to see if your policy automatically covers this equipment or if you need to purchase additional coverage.

A GOOD START

When analyzing your homeowner's insurance coverage, make sure you're carrying insurance to cover the cost of replacing your home today, not when you bought it ten, twenty, or even thirty years ago. One of the biggest mistakes homeowners make is not increasing the total coverage amount on the policy to keep up with building costs today. On the other hand, there's probably no need to include the cost of the land in the insurance. For example, if you paid $300,000 for your home, subtract the value of the lot before figuring out how much insurance you need to carry.

Ask for a Discount

Here are some ideas for getting better coverage for less money: shop around, raise your deductible (the higher the deductible, the cheaper your annual premium), install a home security system, buy your homeowner's and auto policies from the same company, stop smoking, keep your insurance coverage with the same company for half a dozen years or more, and live in the suburbs (which are cheaper to insure than the city). When you're quoted a price, always ask for a discount. The insurance agent might say no, but it never hurts to ask.

EVALUATE YOUR AUTO INSURANCE POLICY

If you drive a car, your state will require you to have automobile insurance.

Where you live, how old you are, the car you drive, and your driving history will affect how much you pay for your car insurance. If you're over twenty-five years of age, you'll pay less than a younger driver will for the same coverage. If you live in the suburbs, you'll pay less than a city dweller will for his or her policy. If you drive a boring car, you'll pay less than if you drive a flashy, expensive car (they're theft targets, as well as being superexpensive to repair). And if you have a great driving record, you'll pay less than if you've had a moving violation in the past three to five years.

The cost for auto insurance coverage has skyrocketed for several reasons: The cost of repairing more sophisticated cars (with all kinds of minicomputers inside of them) has gone up, a larger number of cars are written off as a total loss because it's too expensive to fix them, the medical bills related to accidents have gone up as health costs in general have risen, auto insurance claims are on the rise and more people are suing each other (think road rage), more cars are stolen (some cars types are targeted, like Honda Accords), and cars are just generally more expensive to purchase.

Components of Auto Insurance

Auto insurance is made up of liability, medical payments, uninsured/underinsured motorist, and collision and comprehensive coverage:

Liability. If you hit someone and that person sues you, liability insurance protects you against claims for lost wages, pain and suffering, and property damage. Make sure your policy includes bodily injury liability coverage of at least $100,000 per person and $300,000 per accident. Property-damage liability coverage should be at least $50,000.

Medical payments. If someone gets injured in a crash, there will be medical bills to pay. Your medical coverage pays that bill, regardless of who is at fault in the accident (your personal medical insurance may kick in as well, and the insurance companies will work that out themselves). In states with *no-fault* insurance laws, you can buy *personal injury protection*, which means each driver pays for his or her injuries.

Uninsured/underinsured motorist. If you get hit by someone who isn't insured, or is underinsured for the accident, your coverage pays out. You should make sure this coverage equals your liability, with at least $100,000 per person and $300,000 per accident, at a minimum.

Collision and comprehensive. This part of your insurance pays to fix or replace your car. How much you pay is directly related to the size of your deductible.

Small Business Owners

If your business owns a company car, and your employees will be driving it, ask to purchase a separate auto insurance policy for the company. Don't rely on their personal automobile insurance to cover accidents that happen in a company car on company time.

Nannies, Babysitters, and Other Household Employees

If you have a nanny or babysitter who picks up your children in your car and takes them to school or after-school activities, ask your insurance agent if your auto insurance policy automatically covers them, or if theirs will, in case of an accident. If not, you can typically add adults to your policy with an inexpensive rider.

A GOOD START

When you shop around for auto insurance coverage, the rate you pay for insurance depends on how you combine the different components of your coverage. However, there are several ways to lower your rate:

Use the Internet to shop around. Hundreds of companies offer automobile insurance in every state. Start by checking some of the larger companies, like Geico (www.geico.com) and USAA (www.usaa.com), and insurance portals like Quotesmith (www.quotesmith.com).

Increase your deductible. The easiest way to lower your cost is to raise your deductible (this works with all kinds of insurance, by the way). By doubling your deductible, you may be able to shave your annual premium cost by 5 to 25 percent. (Of course this doesn't always work. I once tried to increase my deductible from $500 to $1,000. The premium for the policy with the $500 deductible was $500, and the premium for the policy with a $1,000 deductible was $493. Typically, the biggest savings will come from upping your deductible from $250 to $500.)

Rethink your coverage for an older car. If your car is worth less than $2,000, you may want to drop collision and comprehensive cost coverage. But understand if you do that and are then in an accident, you won't get a dime toward the purchase of a new car.

Buy a different car. A Ferrari or a Porsche will cost far more to insure than something steady, dependable, and not flashy.

Drive less. If you drive less than 7,500 miles per year per car, your insurance company may give you a break on the cost.

Move to the suburbs. It costs less to insure a car in the suburbs or in the country than it does in the city.

Ask about high-tech discounts. If you've got antilock breaks, automatic seat belts, or air bags, you might get a discount. On the other hand, if you own an SUV with a history of turning over, you might not get one even if it has all the safety bells and whistles on it.

Drive safe. A clean driving record for five years should earn you a discount on your insurance. Accidents and speeding tickets mean your policy will cost you more.

Age-related discounts. You may be eligible if you're over fifty, have had a driver's training course, or if you get good grades (if you're a student).

If you've had an accident or two in the past year, you'll have to look long and hard before you find an insurance company that will cover you. And you'll pay through the nose. But though you may be tempted to forgo insurance in this situation (and just drive safely), don't. If you get into an accident and you don't have insurance, you could be in a lot bigger trouble than being broke. You could wind up in jail. Most states require drivers to purchase auto insurance.

SIMPLE STEP

22

BUY UMBRELLA INSURANCE

In the insurance world, a liability is a situation that could wind up being your financial responsibility. And specific liability coverage is included in most homeowner's, renter's, and auto insurance policies.

But what happens if you're in a horrible automobile accident, which is ruled your fault, and a jury decides you owe the person you hit (or his or her estate, if the person has died as a result of injuries) $1 million? Your automobile insurance has a maximum liability coverage limit of, say, $500,000. You will still owe another $500,000 (not to mention your attorney's fees).

Whatever wealth you've manage to build, win, or inherit will be sucked into this turn of bad luck, and you might even have to declare bankruptcy. You could increase the coverage on all of your individual policies, which will be expensive. An easier and cheaper way is to ask your agent for an *umbrella liability* policy to add to your homeowner's policy.

Also known as *extended personal liability* insurance, umbrella liability protects you from the huge awards juries hand out (you know, the ones that "send a message"). If you have any assets at all to protect (or simply to avoid bankrupting your family in the event of a catastrophe), you should consider purchasing an umbrella policy in excess of $1 million. The policy will protect you and your family from claims stemming from personal activities, so job-related mishaps aren't covered. Premiums are relatively inexpensive. Expect to pay $200 to $300 annually for every $1 million in umbrella liability coverage.

Small Business Owners

Since work-related mishaps and accidents aren't covered under a personal umbrella policy, even if you have an office in your home, you will need to purchase a *business liability* insurance policy. Because work-related injuries can be more costly, consider umbrella liability coverage in excess of $2 million or higher, depending on the nature of your business (i.e., how risky it is) and how many employees you have.

A GOOD START

Since an umbrella policy can simply be added on to your regular homeowner's (or business) insurance coverage, ask your agent to provide you with price quotes for coverage in excess of $1 million. If you have substantial assets, consider an umbrella policy that is roughly equal to or slightly larger than your assets. If you get sued, and the claimant's attorney suspects you have assets, you could be in for a rough ride. The umbrella policy will not only protect you, it should help with the attorney's fees for defending you against a lawsuit.

CONSIDER BUYING LONG-TERM CARE INSURANCE

More than a fourth of all Americans will need some sort of long-term care during their lifetime. The cost for that coverage can easily run more than $150,000 per year (2002 dollars). Round-the-clock home care can cost upward of $4,000 per month. That kind of cash can put a serious crimp into anyone's retirement savings. And if you develop a mentally degenerative disease, like Alzheimer's, you could see your life savings wiped out in a couple of years.

Long-term care insurance is designed to pick up most or all of the bill for your stay in a long-term care facility. The best time to buy long-term care insurance is when you're healthy and in your mid-fifties. The cost for the policy then is relatively inexpensive, but you could pay for the policy for the next twenty or thirty years—which will be expensive, but probably less than the cost of one year in a top-rated long-term care facility.

The real question is, do you actually need the coverage? For folks who have very little in the way of retirement savings, long-term care coverage will probably be too expensive for their budget. If you have oodles of cash saved for your retirement, you can probably afford to pay for the best facility with your own funds. You may choose to pay for a policy simply to avoid spending all your money on your care facility, but you don't need to.

Those who will maximize the financial benefit for long-term care insurance fall somewhere in the middle. If you have some cash in the bank, but not enough to fund two to three years of long-term care for yourself and your spouse or partner (that could run as much as $1 million for two, three-year stays in a long-term care facility), then long-term care insurance is a smart purchase.

A GOOD START

When evaluating policies, be sure to find one that offers you:

- A cost-of-living adjustment (COLA).
- A high enough benefit to cover the cost of a good facility near your friends or family.
- Coverage for three to five years.
- A tax-free policy, if possible. Some long-term care benefits are taxed, others are tax-free. Be sure to ask your agent.
- Lifetime coverage if you have a history of Alzheimer's or other diseases that are debilitative but progress slowly.
- Home health care benefits that aren't limited to skilled care.
- A guarantee that your policy cannot be canceled, declared nonrenewable, or terminated because you get old and sick.
- A thirty-day no-obligation cancellation period.

- No requirement that you first be hospitalized or receive nursing home care in order to qualify for the benefits.

- Some benefits that accrue after so many years (in case you can no longer afford the premiums, you'll get something for all those years of paying into the policy).

By law, long-term care insurers are required to give you a shopper's guide with an outline of coverage that allows easy comparison with other policies. Make sure you get yours. Finally, plan to spend no more than 5 to 7 percent of your annual income on long-term care insurance premiums.

CHECK OUT YOUR COMPANY'S DISABILITY INSURANCE POLICY

The odds that you or your spouse or partner will die when you're young with young kids to support are low. However, the odds that you or your spouse or partner may become disabled and unable to work either for months or years are higher.

Disability insurance replaces up to 70 percent of your income when you have a disability that makes it impossible for you to work. Many companies offer long-term disability coverage (coverage that typically begins sixty to ninety days after the disability occurs). Some even offer short-term disability coverage.

If your employer does not offer any disability coverage, you should consider purchasing long-term disability coverage for yourself, or for the individual who provides most of the income for the family. Keep in mind that you cannot purchase several disability policies in order to "double up" on the benefits. So even if you purchased three disability policies, the most cash you would get is about 70 percent of your predisability income.

A GOOD START

Disability insurance coverage can be complicated and confusing. Here are the main points to consider if you're buying a policy:

What's the definition of disability? You can buy *own-occupation* (pays if you can't work at your specific job), *any-occupation* (pays if you can't work at any job your education and training qualify you for, from the insurer's perspective), or *income-replacement* (covers the difference between what you earned prior to the disability and now) insurance. Do you have to be completely or partially disabled to receive benefits? Does your policy include *presumptive disability* (you are presumed fully disabled and entitled to full benefits if you lose your sight, speech, hearing, etc.)?

How big are the benefits? Typically, you are limited to sixty to eighty percent of your predisability income. Higher-income workers tend to get less. The average is seventy percent.

When do payments start? When you buy your own policy, you get to choose when to begin your payments. The longer you wait, the cheaper the policy. The minimum wait is thirty days before the benefits kick in, but you'll pay a lot more than if you wait one hundred eighty days for payments to start.

When does the money stop? You can buy insurance that will pay for a year, two years, five years, to age sixty-seven, or throughout your lifetime. But if you'll receive a pension from your employer, have substantial retirement savings, or will inherit a chunk of cash someday, you shouldn't pay for lifetime coverage because you may not need the money once you reach retirement age.

Does it include cost-of-living adjustments (COLA)? Make sure your benefits at least keep up with inflation.

Can the policy be cancelled? With a noncancellable policy, as long as you pay your premiums on time the insurer can't raise your rates or bump you. A guaranteed renewable policy means you'll be renewed but could receive rate increases.

When do the premiums get waived? Once you file a claim, you may be able to stop paying your premium. Be sure to check with your agent.

What happens after? Is there an option to buy additional coverage without evidence of insurability at a later date? What happens to your policy? If you sit out two years with a long-term disability but are then able to go back to work, will your policy cover you again? Or will you need a new policy?

What types of jobs aren't covered by disability insurance? If you're a writer, for example, you're basically uninsurable by private disability insurance. But if you join a nonprofit association that offers a wide range of insurance programs to members, you may be able to purchase affordable coverage that way. Make sure the disability coverage is job specific. For example, if you're an attorney and can no longer be an attorney for whatever reason (even if you can be a salesperson), you'll still be covered by your policy and will receive benefits. Your agent, or the benefits coordinator at the nonprofit association through which you'll purchase your insurance, should have more details.

BUY FLOOD INSURANCE

If you live in a federally designated flood plain (and you can check with your local municipality for flood plain information—don't rely on the seller's agent to tell you), and you get a mortgage, your lender will require you to purchase flood insurance.

Flood insurance for homes located in flood plains is backed by the U.S. government. The policies are sold by insurance agents. The average annual cost is about $300 for $100,000 worth of flood insurance. The maximum amount of coverage is $250,000, though you can purchase policies privately in excess of that amount (covered by private insurers, not the federal government).

If you buy flood insurance, however, that doesn't mean everything in your home will be covered under the policy. Typically, finished basements are not covered by federal flood insurance policies, except for basics like the washer, dryer, furnace, and air-conditioning units. You'll take a loss (unless you buy supplemental coverage) on any damaged carpeting and wood paneling, not to mention items you may have stored in your basement.

The cost of your policy depends on the value of your home, construction costs, and where your home is located. If it's close to a shoreline, you'll pay a lot more money for your policy than if you live several hundred yards away.

For the money, flood insurance is about the cheapest kind of insurance you can purchase, and it's well worth the few hundred bucks you'll spend on the policy. A big mistake homeowners make is thinking their regular homeowner's insurance policy will cover flooding. It won't. In fact, anything that floods because of a "rising body of water," including an eighteen-inch rainstorm, won't be covered. About the only flooding coverage you'll get is damage caused by a burst pipe.

I recently received a letter from a reader. After living in her home for fifteen years, she received a letter from her lender. The letter informed the homeowner that her home is now located in a federally designated flood plain, and she needs to purchase flood insurance.

"That's silly," she wrote in her letter. "I live at the top of a hill in my community, about 50 feet above the nearest running water."

The homeowner wanted to know if flood plains can be changed and, if so, did she really have to buy flood insurance.

The answer is yes, and yes. Federally designated flood plains can be adjusted, enlarged, or shrunk depending on new surveys that are drawn. You can check with your local city or village government to find out if your home is located in a flood plain. However, even if you are in a new flood plain, you may be able to escape purchasing flood insurance if your home is high enough.

What you'll need to do is to hire a surveyor to see if your home is far enough above the flood plain to qualify for an exemption. The surveyor will charge maybe $1,000 or more, but you'll easily make that back by not paying for flood insurance. (Check with your lender to make sure it will accept a surveyor's report. If not, ask if the lender has a procedure by which you can prove you are not located in a flood zone.)

A GOOD START

Though it's cheap and easily available, only 20 percent of homeowners who live in a flood plain have flood insurance. Many people believe the federal government will pick up the tab if a river overflows and sweeps away their home. Not true! The government may make a low-interest loan available to you, but that's all it is—a loan. You'll lose everything in your home, and you'll still owe whatever cash you owed to the lender on your mortgage. (And what will your land be worth once it's swept clean by a flood? Not much.)

For details and referrals to an insurance agent who sells flood insurance, call the Federal Emergency Management Agency (commonly known as FEMA, 800-427-4661) or check out the agency's Web site at www.fema.gov.

CONSIDER BUYING
EARTHQUAKE INSURANCE

Unlike flood insurance, earthquake insurance is offered through private insurers, typically as an added coverage (also called an *endorsement*) to your policy. But the frequent, damaging earthquakes experienced in California during the 1990s has made this insurance coverage difficult to buy and very expensive.

Many insurance companies either pulled out of the earth-quake insurance business or decided to limit the areas in which it would be offered (a practice known as *redlining*, since insurance companies used to outline areas in red markers in which certain types of coverage wouldn't be sold). Between the cost and the coverage areas, just 10 per-cent of homeowners living in areas that could be affected by an earthquake have earthquake insurance.

You can purchase earthquake insurance through your insurance agent. In California (where by law it must be offered by insurance companies doing business in the state), it is reasonably easy to get, but very expensive, depending on whether or not you live close to or on a fault line, what type of home you have, and whether the structure of your home incorporates modern antiearthquake technology. In some areas of the country (other than California) that are highly seismic, coverage for earthquake damage may not be available at any price.

A GOOD START

Because earthquake insurance is very expensive (some people I know pay thousands of dollars a year for their policy), many homeowners opt to self-insure. They put the cost of the insurance (thousands of dollars a year) into a savings account or money market account and hope that if an earthquake strikes, their home will sustain only minor damage, which they'll pay to repair from their savings.

If you're moving to an area prone to earthquakes, it's possible to hire a structural engineer to assess the potential damage an earthquake would have on your property. It's worth the several hundred dollars you'll spend to see how much damage your home would sustain. From there, you can estimate the repair costs.

If you live on a hill or mountain, or by a ravine, you may wish to purchase mudslide insurance as a rider to your homeowner's policy. This coverage will protect you if during a huge rainstorm your home is swept away by mud cascading down the hill.

CHECK OUT YOUR
HEALTH INSURANCE POLICY

Although some 40 million Americans don't have health insurance, most of us do have at least some catastrophic coverage. Many employers provide health insurance for their full-time employees, which you help pay for with dollars deducted from your paycheck. If you're buying health insurance on your own, you'll want to look at four numbers: the deductible, the total amount of coverage per person, the annual cost, and the maximum lifetime limit.

Most policies allow you to decide how high a deductible (the amount you pay before the insurance coverage kicks in) you'll pay each year. If you choose a low deductible, say $150, you'll pay a higher annual premium because the policy will kick in sooner. If you choose a higher deductible, say $1,000, you'll pay for more up front but you'll keep your annual premium lower. Which way should you go? If you're healthy and you can afford it, choose a higher deductible. You'll have a lower annual premium and may save a few dollars over the course of the year. If you have kids, who tend to rack up a lot of doctor visits, perhaps you'll want to choose a lower deductible, so the insurance kicks in sooner.

Health insurance is really catastrophic insurance. It covers the little things (once you've hit the deductible), but it really pays off in the event of a life-threatening illness.

Could you afford the $100,000 (or more) cost of a heart-lung transplant? Few people have that kind of cash on hand. And that's why we buy insurance. But getting to the maximum limit of a policy is easier these days than you can imagine. If you're buying insurance, check out the maximum limit. Try to buy a policy with a $5 million (or higher) lifetime limit per person.

Finally, make sure you can afford the annual cost of the policy, because insurance costs only go up. As I was writing this book, my insurance carrier hiked the cost of my annual premium by 18 percent. Several years ago I went through a two-year period where my insurer raised the premium every six months to cover losses elsewhere.

If your health insurance is getting too expensive for you, and you're relatively healthy, you can either change plans (from a PPO to an HMO, for example) or change insurance companies. If that's not an option, consider raising your deductible.

A GOOD START

Some insurance companies require that you call them within twenty-four hours of being admitted to the emergency room. If you fail to do so, you may end up owing a larger share of the medical bills. They may require a preauthorization before any expensive medical test, such as a colonoscopy. If you forget to precertify, the bill may be yours to pay. Read the fine print to know what your obligations are.

Also, if you have a chronic medical problem, like diabetes, wear an ID bracelet. Not only will medical professionals be able to administer life-saving drugs more quickly, but you may end up saving yourself money in the long run.

Finally, some insurance companies offer *dread disease* insurance, which pays out if you get a specific illness, like cancer. I think the cost you pay for these specific medical insurance policies is too high. Skip them and make sure your regular insurance policy gives you adequate coverage.

It's tough to find the right medical coverage at the right price. Thanks to the Internet, searching for medical insurance is getting easier. Start by checking out Insure.com, a Web site devoted to information about the insurance industry. There are links there to various insurers and plans. Also try Quotesmith.com, which offers a variety of different types of insurance for sale as well. (I've bought term life insurance through Quotesmith. It's underwritten by a first-class company and the experience was practically painless.) Finally, consider doing a search for medical insurance through a search portal like Google.com.

LADDER YOUR TERM
LIFE INSURANCE POLICIES

If you have people who depend on your income, or if you and your children depend on someone else's income to provide you with the basic necessities of life, then you probably need to purchase life insurance.

There are two basic types of life insurance: term and whole life. The word "term" means the insurance policy covers you for a specific period of time, usually a year. If you die within the covered period, your insurance policy will pay the named beneficiaries. Term insurance is often sold for a level load, that is, the premium you pay can be fixed for a number of years, say fifteen, twenty, twenty-five, or even thirty years. So if you choose to pay $500 for a $500,000 term life insurance premium, and you choose a thirty-year level load period, you'll never pay more than $500 per year for the next thirty years for the same policy. (But if you stop paying the premium, your insurance policy will end.)

Unfortunately, most insurance brokers want to sell you a version of whole life insurance rather than a term policy. Why? Because whole life insurance policies, which include "variable" life policies, "universal variable" life policies, and any other kind of life insurance other than term, include fat commissions for insurance brokers and hefty management fees for the company.

Here's how a whole life policy works: You combine insurance with savings. The upfront commission is typically equal to at least a year's premium, and sometimes two, making these policies extremely expensive from the get-go.

Each year, you pay more than you'd have to for the death benefit only, with the extra going toward the savings part of the policy. Brokers trying to sell you a whole life policy will show you charts that suggest that all the extra money you pay in will eventually pay up the policy so you won't have to put anything more in to get the death benefit. Sounds good, right? Except that if the stock market doesn't produce 11 to 15 percent annual returns, it will never happen. And given the ups and downs in the stock market during the past decade, it's unlikely that you'll ever get the benefit of these "vanishing premiums." But don't expect your broker to tell you that!

Now nearing eighty, Angie had bought a whole life policy a decade earlier. Although she had earned a sizeable amount of money from selling her home and an investment property, she wanted to have some sort of insurance so that she'd leave her children an inheritance. An insurance agent "sold" her on the concept of "vanishing premiums," and so for years she paid more than $1,000 per month toward her whole life policy.

Eight years into it, she was astonished to get a bill for another year's worth of premiums. When she called her agent, he told her there had been a mistake. When she received another bill the next year, she did some investigation. Not only would there never be a "vanishing premium" with her policy (the real world stock returns hadn't quite caught up with the promises the agent made), but the agent had dipped into the policy savings to pay for the premium the previous year—without informing Angie. Once she found out how these policies really worked, Angie cashed out and cancelled the policy.

Because whole life policies are so expensive, it's difficult to buy enough coverage to protect your family. And the entire point of life insurance is to provide your survivors with enough cash to continue in the lifestyle you'd want them to have.

What should you do? Buy term insurance and ladder your policies. If you buy term insurance, you can buy a twenty-five-year level load policy. Five years later you can buy another term insurance policy with another twenty-five-year level load policy (don't give up paying the premium for the first term insurance policy). If you need even more coverage, you can buy a third term insurance policy, with a twenty-five-year level load.

The end result is that you'll have thirty-five years' worth of term insurance coverage, with all three policies running for a fifteen-year period in the middle, hopefully when your expenses of raising your children will be the heaviest:

Policy A for $250,000 runs from year one through year twenty-five

Policy B for $250,000 runs from year five through year thirty

Policy C for $250,000 runs from year ten through year thirty-five

If you get married and buy your first term policy in year one, and then have children in years three and five, your second policy (Policy B) will coincide with the birth of your second child. Over the next five years you'll have $500,000 in coverage. When your children are five and seven, Policy C kicks in and for the next fifteen years (until your children are twenty and twenty-two), you will have $750,000 in life insurance, should something happen. Then, for the next five years, you'll have $500,000 in insurance, and for the final five years you'll have just $250,000 in coverage. By the time the final policy is through, your children will be thirty and thirty-two years of age—old enough (we hope) to take care of themselves.

Why is it cheaper to buy term insurance than whole life insurance? There's a tremendous amount of competition in the term life insurance business. For example, you might pay just $250 per year for $250,000 in term insurance benefits. With whole life insurance, you might pay $250 per month (although some of that goes to pay commission and into your savings).

Small Business Owners

If you want to buy a life insurance policy for your employees, you will typically be limited to providing a year or two of salary for each employee. Check with your insurance agent for details. If you're thinking of having your company buy a policy for you, be aware that there may be tax consequences of doing so. For example, if you (personally) buy a life insurance policy, the benefits will be tax-free, though possibly not estate tax-free (it depends on the size of your estate). However, if your corporation or company purchases the policy, your estate may have to pay income tax on the benefits before it passes through your estate. Then, you may owe estate taxes. You could be taxed twice on the funds. Ask your accountant for help sorting through various options.

A GOOD START

You can't buy life insurance until you know what your family's short-term and long-term expenses will be. Here's a worksheet that will help you figure out how much life insurance you need to buy:

How Much Life Insurance Do You Need? Worksheet

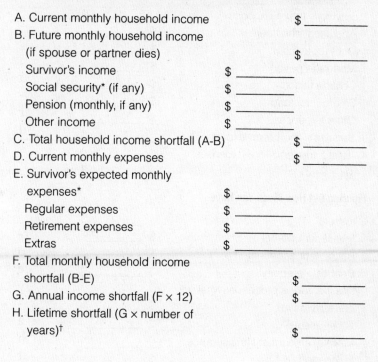

A. Current monthly household income $ _____

B. Future monthly household income
(if spouse or partner dies) $ _____

    Survivor's income $ _____

    Social security* (if any) $ _____

    Pension (monthly, if any) $ _____

    Other income $ _____

C. Total household income shortfall (A-B) $ _____

D. Current monthly expenses $ _____

E. Survivor's expected monthly
expenses* $ _____

    Regular expenses $ _____

    Retirement expenses $ _____

    Extras $ _____

F. Total monthly household income
shortfall (B-E) $ _____

G. Annual income shortfall (F × 12) $ _____

H. Lifetime shortfall (G × number of
years)† $ _____

---

*Some experts and Internet calculators assume that when a spouse or partner dies, your remaining expenses will be just 75 percent of what they were when your spouse or partner was alive. Often, the expenses will be the same or greater (things get more expensive due to inflation). Be sure to factor in these possibilities. I've always felt it's better to overestimate than not have enough in a crisis.

†The lifetime shortfall is the amount of missing cash in each year's budget multiplied by the number of years you'll need the extra income—typically until the last child is through with college.

Additional Expenses

I. Survivor's future expenses‡ $ _____

    Additional child care $ _____

    Debt repayment $ _____

    Mortgage payoff $ _____

    College tuition $ _____

    Emergency fund $ _____

    Other expenses $ _____

J. Survivor's short-term expenses§ $ _____

K. Total future and final expenses

    (H + I + J) $ _____

Figuring Out How Much You Have

L. Assets $ _____

    Investment portfolio $ _____

    Retirement accounts $ _____

    Real estate equity $ _____

    Life insurance proceeds (what you

    currently have) $ _____

    Other assets $ _____

    M. Total amount of life insurance

        needed (K-L) $ _____

---

‡Future expenses are how much it will cost you to live going forward.

§The survivor's final expenses include the cost of funeral services. The average funeral costs $5,000, though experts advise doubling that number to be safe. If your spouse or partner dies intestate (without a will), tack on another $10,000 for probate and other legal expenses and fees.

Investments

ACTIVELY MANAGE YOUR MONEY

So many of us lead such busy lives, we may think hiring a money manager or a financial planner or an estate attorney is the answer to keeping our financial lives in order.

And for some people, especially those who have accumulated significant assets, a financial planner or money manager might be an important way to start getting your money organized and invested correctly. An estate attorney can help develop a plan for managing and giving away your assets.

So we think about scheduling appointments, and we start talking to our friends about who they're using and if they like those people, and all of this "research" gets slotted around work, vacations, taking the kids to soccer practice, and the rest of the swarm of activities we're involved with each day.

Before you know it, six months or a year, or perhaps more, has flown by and nothing has been done. Your cash has continued to accumulate wherever it was you left it, probably in a savings account, earning just about next to nothing.

Which wouldn't be so bad except that some people don't even know where their savings account is. Really! Even if you're a huge celebrity with a manager on staff who pays your monthly bills, there's no excuse for you not knowing where every one of your dollars is invested. We spend too much time and effort earning our salaries and building up our nest eggs to be so laid back about where we put that money. And if a crisis hits before you get your financial act together, not knowing where your money is could make a bad situation a whole lot worse.

Actively managing your money doesn't mean you have to spend all day watching the ticker roll by on CNBC or CNN. It doesn't mean you have to have a subscription to the *Wall Street Journal* or *Barron's*. And it doesn't mean you have to balance your checkbook on the day you receive your statement (although that's always a good idea).

Actively managing your money means that you know what you have, what it's worth, where it's at, and what, if any, penalties you'll pay when you liquidate it. Actively managing your money means at least twice a year, you and your spouse or partner sit down and figure out whether your short-term and long-term financial goals are being met. Actively managing your money means making investment decisions based on logic, reason, and research, rather than on hot tips from cold calls or conversations around the water cooler.

When you actively manage your money, it makes you feel as though you're really in control. A television journalist I know has spent the past six months taking simple steps toward being in active control of her money. (She is using another book I wrote, *50 Simple Things You Can Do to Improve Your Personal Finances*, as a guide.) She gives me weekly updates as to how things are going. For years she was waiting for her husband to take charge, and one day decided she could do it herself. She went from not knowing what she was spending to being in complete control of her finances. Today she exudes confidence. I think the confidence comes from knowing that, thanks to a lot of hard work, her financial life is in good shape, and continuing to get healthier and stronger.

A GOOD START

Do you know how much money you spend in a given week, month, or year? Do you know what companies your mutual funds are invested in? Do you know how much money your investments are generating?

Many of the Simple Steps in this book will help you get your finances under control. In order to make the lists of assets and contact names I've suggested, you'll have to know where these assets are and how to access them. But knowing how much you earn and how much you spend is another matter.

Buy a cheap little notebook. Now write down every cent you spend for a month (including the cost of the notebook). If your spouse or partner normally does the grocery shopping, pickups at the dry cleaners, and runs to the drugstore, change places and handle the daily purchases for a while. Everyone should know how much a bag of groceries costs and what it really takes to feed your family.

Writing down what you spend will help you find ways to plug your budget. But there's another reason to do it—writing down what you spend helps you take mental control of your money. It forces you to think about your income and expenses every time cash leaves your pocket.

An attorney friend of mine says he doesn't care what he spends as long as he maintains a positive balance in his checking account. In fact, I know several people who live their lives that way. The problem with that approach is that you're not in control. If you want to spend money, and you have it to spend, fine. But it's much better to make that decision from a point of knowledge. For example, if you order out four times per week at forty dollars for dinner for four, I want you to understand that it costs you an extra $160 (or whatever the number), which could translate to a savings of some $7,500 per year—and that's before you earn interest on your money.

Life is about choices, and managing your money is one decision after another. Actively making those decisions leads to a lifelong understanding of how you relate to money and how it can buy you some things and not others.

Until a crisis hits, the ability to actively manage your finances just makes things like taxes and keeping your credit clean easier. But once disaster strikes, the ability to actively manage your finances, which you'd already gotten under control, can save you thousands of dollars. If you need to put the brakes on spending, years of writing down every cent you spend (Quicken or Microsoft Money are excellent, easy ways to track your spending) will enable you to easily decide what you can cut out of the budget. If you're in control of what you're spending and investing, you can make an intelligent decision about investing an inheritance, paying or financing large medical expenses, and even refinancing your home.

Actively managing your money makes your financial life run better every day. But in a crisis, the ability to do so will pay off big-time.

SIMPLE STEP
30

DIVERSIFY YOUR PORTFOLIO

In times of national crisis, such as a recession, war, or acts of terrorism, the stock market can fluctuate wildly.

As my grandfather used to say, it doesn't matter what happens to your portfolio unless you're going to sell. Buying and selling stocks, bonds, and mutual funds is a long-term business, and you hope and expect that over time, say five to forty years, the market will continue to go up in a steady fashion (with highs and lows along the way).

Most investment analysts recommend that you diversify your portfolio, that is, spread it around to different types of investments that will hopefully move out of synch with each other in case of a market downturn. For example, rarely do technology, biotech, energy, and real estate companies grow or contract at exactly the same rate. By spreading the risk around and investing in a wide variety of companies, you're lowering the risk that you could lose everything in a downturn.

In a Personal Crisis

Personal financial crises are often brought on by economic problems. Commonly, lots of people lose their jobs in a recession. If you lose your job, the last thing you want is for your assets to be hit hard because of a stock market dive related to an economic downturn. By investing in a wide variety of stocks or mutual funds, you hedge your bets.

Similarly, if you unexpectedly inherit a large amount of money, you should invest it in a conservatively diversified portfolio while you consider your next step. When my friend Pam lost her husband, her brother Tom (an estate attorney) invested the insurance money conservatively, in a diversified portfolio of stocks and bonds. During the first three years, the stock market tumbled, but Pam's nest egg didn't lose that much of its value thanks to the diversification. When Pam is ready to make a different investment choice, or if she opts to keep the money where it is, she will be far better off than had she put her money in mutual funds that were aggressively focused on the "hot" stock or fund of the day.

A GOOD START

The key to successfully diversifying your portfolio is to first know what you have. Make a list of all of your stocks, bonds, and the top ten companies owned by each of your mutual funds. If you don't know what companies your mutual fund currently holds, you can check it out online at Morningstar.com or go to the Web site of your mutual fund company and look it up. At last resort, call and ask the company to send you a copy of their prospectus and fund holdings (something you should have received before you invested).

Once you know what companies you own (through mutual funds or individually), you can research the companies and the industries in which they operate. For example, Mobil-Exxon is an energy company; Amgen is a biotech company that creates and makes various drugs. Many Web sites, plus Quicken and Microsoft Money software, will allow you to list your stocks and automatically sort them into industries and categories for you.

A conservatively diversified portfolio will keep some of your assets in stocks, some in bonds, the rest in cash. Depending on how old you are and how much risk you want to take, you might put 70 percent of your assets in stocks or mutual funds, 20 percent in bonds, and 10 percent in cash. If you want to be a shade more aggressive, you might try 80 percent stocks, 10 percent bonds, and 10 percent cash. But within your stock holdings, you'll want diversification as well. Consider putting most of your money into large-cap (the biggest companies with the largest capitalization) stocks, with some going into small and mid-cap companies, and another portion (much smaller) into foreign companies.

One of the biggest mistakes we make with our finances is to put too much cash into a single company—especially if it is the company that employs us. You should put no more than 10 percent of your total investable assets (minus your home) in any one company's stock. Resist the temptation to buy too much company stock. If you can buy it at a discount, consider selling some of your holdings to diversify into other investments before you buy more.

When the former energy trading giant Enron collapsed at the end of 2001, a lot of ink was spent explaining why current and former employees of the company had nothing in their retirement portfolios. Many of these employees had 50, 60, 80, and even 90 percent of their retirement funds in Enron stock.

When the stock fell from a high of 90 to nothing within a few months, only a few employees were lucky enough to have sold the stock (at whatever price) and left the funds in cash. The rest of the employees watched their paper profits go up in a puff of smoke.

It's an extreme example, but a telling one. Although some of the Enron stock employees held in their retirement accounts was restricted (that is, it couldn't be sold until the employees had reached the age of 50), much of it was sellable. But why sell the stock of the seventh largest company in America? Especially when management seems so positive on the long-term future of the company?

It's a tough call to make. Many companies seem solid and well managed. And if you're working for a company, you may feel you'd know if something was going on. Apparently, some companies aren't as solid as they appear to be, and when that's the case a company can go under virtually overnight. Good-bye retirement! While many of Microsoft's employees became millionaires thanks to the stock they received when they joined the company, more companies suffer Enron's fate, and the employees end up with nothing.

The safest thing to do is to develop a strategy to diversify your holdings on a regular basis, no matter where the price of the company's stock is on that particular day. If you have more than 10 percent of your retirement assets in your company's stock, sell some on the first day of every quarter. Or, if you are permitted to buy stock at a discount, sell some of the other stock that has appreciated. A 10 or 15 percent profit is far better than losing principle.

Diversifying your retirement cash isn't sexy. And it isn't necessarily something you'll want to brag about at the water cooler. But it sure could help you sleep at night.

SIMPLE STEP
31

UPDATE YOUR BENEFICIARIES IN YOUR RETIREMENT PLANS AND LIFE INSURANCE POLICIES

Over the years that I have been reporting on real estate and money matters, I have received maybe a dozen letters from readers describing the same terrible situation: A spouse or partner died, and instead of the survivor receiving the insurance money or the proceeds from the deceased's IRA or 401(k), it went to a former spouse simply because the named beneficiary on the account was never updated.

What many people don't understand is that even if you have a will, the named beneficiary will take precedence in terms of distribution of assets after death. So if you don't remove your ex's name from your life insurance policy, even if you specifically name the beneficiary in your will, the courts will ignore that legal document and the life insurance proceeds will go to the person named as beneficiary in the policy.

I can't stress how important it is to make sure the named beneficiaries of your life insurance policies, retirement accounts, and other accounts are the individuals, charities, or nonprofit organizations you would choose today. It's especially important if you die intestate, that is, without a will. If you die intestate, the state's probate court will determine who receives your assets. If you die intestate and you have no named beneficiaries on your insurance policies and retirement accounts, the court may hand out your assets in a way you wouldn't have wished.

A GOOD START

Go through your insurance policies, retirement accounts, pension accounts, investment accounts, annuities, and any other accounts or policies that allow you to name a beneficiary. See who is listed as the beneficiary, and then change the beneficiary to reflect your wishes today. Check your beneficiaries every few years, or when a major event happens in your life: You marry or divorce, a child is born, a loved one dies, you change jobs, or you move. These are the times you want to make sure your estate is in order.

Typically, companies will allow you to name a primary beneficiary and a contingent beneficiary (in case something happens to the primary beneficiary). The primary beneficiary can actually be two or more individuals, and you can decide how much you want each of them to receive (it can be 50/50 or 90/10, depending on what you want). Likewise, the contingent beneficiary can be two or more people and you can also decide what percentage share you'd like them to have.

Frequently, a spouse will name his or her spouse or partner as the primary beneficiary and their children as the contingent beneficiaries. What happens if the primary and contingent beneficiaries die together? That depends on state law. If a family dies together, state law determines who died first (for example, the father might be deemed to have died first, followed by the spouse and then the children), so the money might pass into the primary beneficiary's estate. Talk to a local estate planner or attorney to find out what your state law says about beneficiaries and inheritances.

If you don't have a copy of your policy listing the beneficiaries handy, call your insurance company or investment firm to ask who is named. If you need to make a change, the company should have a form that will allow you to rename the beneficiary on the account.

Leonora recently decided to check on the beneficiaries of her own and her husband's life insurance policies. Once she figured out where the policies were (it took some time to gather up the documents), she realized that her husband hadn't changed the beneficiary on his first life insurance policy—his mother. While Leonora knew her mother-in-law would have given her back the insurance money, she thought it important that her husband make the decision about whether he wanted to keep the beneficiary of that policy the way it was, or change it to Leonora, or their two children. When she talked to her husband, he said he thought he had changed the beneficiary on the policy years earlier—but apparently he hadn't.

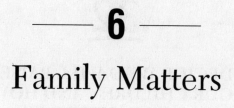

6

Family Matters

SIMPLE STEP
32

DECIDE WHO WILL RAISE YOUR CHILDREN AND HOW, IF YOU CAN'T DO IT

There can't be any more depressing conversation to have with your spouse or loved ones than who will raise your children if something happens to you both. Losing one parent is tough enough, but losing both parents means children may not only lose their sense of parental and emotional stability, but will likely have to move from their home as well.

Choosing the right person, or family, is extremely difficult, especially since the people who may give the most emotionally to your children may not have the financial acumen to manage their inheritance successfully. The happiest, most well-adjusted children could end up with the biggest spendthrifts in the family. Will they blow your children's inheritance on trinkets and toys but give them a loving support system? Or will they be excellent money managers, creating great wealth for your children, but not give them a warm shoulder to cry on?

Why can't you have both? Perhaps you have a family member who can both raise children as you'd raise them and be financially savvy. But in many families, hard choices have to be made. And the decision you make will have lasting repercussions on both your children and their financial status.

A GOOD START

Make a list of every family member who qualifies as a potential guardian for your kids. Ideally, you'd want someone who has the time, ability, and desire to take on your children and the lasting nightmare your untimely death will create for them. It's also helpful if the family is financially stable. You don't want them to see your children as a financial windfall, nor do you want them to see your children as a financial liability.

Next, make a list of the qualities that are most important: How your children respond to these family members or friends is crucial, as is how they've raised or are raising their own children. Do you want the family to live in your neighborhood? Would they need to move to a bigger home to accommodate your family? Do you have too many children for one family to take on? What is the financial status of the family? Do they earn enough to pay the incidentals involved with raising children or would the cash you leave behind be tapped for every expense? Do they share your religious beliefs? Are their emotional or financial resources already strained by their own children?

Don't worry about whose feelings will be hurt if they are not chosen for this important mission. Instead, focus on the family your children will be happiest with just in case. If you have to make a choice between a family that will support your children emotionally and one that can do the right thing financially, choose the happiness of your children. You can compensate for poor financial management by purchasing more life insurance and appointing someone else to take on the inheritance management duties, if you have to.

When you've outlined all of the possibilities, it should be easy to eliminate most of the names on your list for one reason or another. Perhaps you're committed to raising children in the town in which you live and won't send them out of state. Or, perhaps you know a family who already has a sick child and taking on your children would push them too far. Or, perhaps your sibling is unmarried and shows poor judgment in his or her choice of dates. Or, your parents are too old to take on babies and raise them (though some grandparents who end up raising their grandchildren have done beautifully). Or, a family doesn't have the same religious beliefs you have.

Separating Money Management from Child Rearing

If you feel you need another pair of eyes to help oversee your children's inheritance, ask another family member to help. You can work with your estate attorney (see Chapter 7) to set up a trust for your children naming both the guardian and the other family member as trustees for the account. You can set a limit on how much can be spent per month from the trust for regular expenses, with extra expenses being approved by both trustees. If you want more or less control of the inheritance, you can place tighter and more specific restrictions on the use of the trust funds.

But be careful in tying the hands of the guardians too tightly, financial experts warn. If they're raising your children, you want them to have enough money to do what you would have wanted with your children. You don't want them to have to fight the other relatives for every nickel, because that could wear the guardians down.

Once you've made your decision, you have to ask the prospective guardian if he or she would be willing to raise your children in the event something happened to you and your partner. This is a hard question to ask, and don't be surprised if the individual or family you've asked requests some additional time to consider it. Agreeing to take on another family's children isn't an easy decision, financially or emotionally.

If you're going to ask someone else to oversee the financial management and investment of your children's inheritance, you should ask that individual if he or she is willing to take on this enormous responsibility. You should also be up front about that, too, with the prospective guardian. Say, "I'm asking Uncle Rich to help manage the investment of the money, so that you'll have enough to raise our children the way you raise your own."

It may take a village to raise a child, but someone has to be in charge. Still, if you want more relatives to help, ask them. You may be surprised by their answer.

Again, these are very difficult conversations to have and even tougher decisions to make. Just remember this: If you don't decide, a court that has no understanding at all of your family structure or relationships will make a decision that could make life difficult, if not impossible, for your precious children.

DECIDE WHO WILL CARE FOR YOU
IF YOU CAN'T

You don't want people who have no emotional interest in your family to make decisions that will govern your health care (or that of your spouse or partner) in the event of an accident, serious injury, or illness. For that reason, it's important to decide (while you're mentally able) who will care for you and your spouse or partner if you are unable to do it yourself.

Legally, the best way to do this will be to sign a document called a *power of attorney for health care* or a *durable power of attorney for health matters.* I'll discuss what this document is and what it can do for you in Simple Step 40. But for now it's important to make the decision as to who that person, or family, will be, and to contemplate the ramifications of your choice.

A GOOD START

How should you decide? Start by taking a look at who may have the time and resources to oversee your health care. It may be a child, if your children are grown, or a sibling. In one family, the eldest daughter built a wheelchair-accessible addition onto her home, just in case her mother (who is perfectly able to live alone now) needed it. Soon after it was finished, the mother spent a week living in "her" new room, recovering from surgery. In another family, a son moved in with his nearly century-old mother for half the year, in order to help make her life easier. By all accounts, his care and nurturing has kept his mother alive and well for the past eight years.

The person you choose to help care for you (or your spouse or partner) should have the ability to make tough decisions. If you have a living will that calls for no heroic measures to be taken to keep you alive after a devastating blow to your health, the person you choose needs to have the emotional resources to implement your will. Likewise, if you decide every effort must be made to keep you alive, the person you've chosen must be able to fight for that as well.

Financially, you'll want to choose someone who can work with whomever has the power of attorney for your financial matters. If there is fighting between these individuals, your assets may not be used to pay necessary financial bills, which could compromise your health.

On the other hand, if you give a power of attorney for health care and financial matters to the same person, you have to trust that this individual will do the right thing, and spend whatever it takes to keep you alive for as long as possible, if that is your wish, even if it means spending his or her inheritance.

TEACH YOUR CHILDREN HOW TO MANAGE MONEY WHEN THEY'RE YOUNG

When my son Alex was born, he received three piggy banks from various members of our extended family. Was it his mother's line of work or his father's conservative nature that inspired the gifts? We'll never know.

Just after his first birthday, we took the opportunity to talk to Alex about his piggy banks and the change he could keep in them. A few years later my mother-in-law brought back metal boxes with coin slits at the top. The boxes were filled with chocolate candy that was soon eaten. But the "banks" have provided years of entertainment for Alex and his brother Michael, both of whom keep foreign and domestic coins inside.

I suppose you don't know until they're grown up whether your children will respect money or be enslaved by it. Will they be spendthrifts or hoarders? Fiscally imprudent or conservative? Will they know how to create wealth or simply waste every opportunity?

My husband and I have high hopes that our children will know the value of a dollar. But we work at it every single day. On a visit to the grocery store, the children can elect to spend some of their money to buy a treat, but they usually don't. When we went to see the circus, Alex wanted a program filled with color photos of the attractions—but not enough to actually spend some of his savings. What we're trying to teach them is that we have enough money to provide the staples in life—food, clothing, shelter, and education—but not enough to waste on junk and toys. What you do with your money requires tough choices every day.

What I have seen, through my years of writing about money and interviewing both parents and their children, is that the younger your children are when you start teaching them to appreciate how hard it is to earn a living—and how much, with careful planning, those dollars can buy—the easier it will be for them to understand the true nature and meaning of money.

Raising fiscally responsible children is even more important when you consider what could happen in a family crisis.

As the moral of the story says, it's far easier to go from being poor to being rich than rich to poor. If you should lose your job, lose your spouse or partner, or develop a life-threatening illness, you'll probably need to cut your budget, even if you're as prepared as possible. If up until that moment your children always received everything they asked for, the memories of their former "rich" life could haunt them. If they've learned the value of judicious spending, it could inspire them.

Raising fiscally responsible children is another way of preparing them to deal with the crises they will face in their own lives. Whether it's paying for their own college or post-graduate education, financing their first home, paying for their own wedding, or perhaps dealing with their own job loss, knowing how to manage their money is the best gift you can give your children. It will also stand you in good stead when looking to give your power of attorney for financial matters to someone responsible.

A GOOD START

For a book I wrote several years ago, *100 Questions You Should Ask About Your Personal Finances,* I interviewed dozens of college students. Some had sky-high credit card debts, others had none. Some were paying for their own college education, others won scholarships or their parents were footing the bill. But all of them said they learned how to manage (or mismanage) money from their parents. The ones with credit card debt said their parents either lived beyond their means or they actively chose to ignore the lesson, figuring they could pay it off once they got a job (they forgot about rent, car payments, food, entertainment, and the other things that come out of a monthly paycheck).

Here are a few simple tips for raising financially aware children:

- Don't give your children every toy, game, CD, CD-ROM, and treat they ask for. Give them either/or choices that reward the deferred treat.

- Give your children a weekly allowance as early as you feel they understand the concept. Some people give their children their grade year plus a dollar. (If they have to pay for the cost of transportation or lunch, then the amount is adjusted). So a kindergartener would get a dollar and a first-grader would get two dollars.

- Make participating in the general household a condition of the allowance. Children should be expected to keep their rooms relatively tidy and make their beds. Our kids have to keep the basement clean and their toys put away. Assign chores as you see fit, but assign something.

- Extra chores should be rewarded. Some families pay their children to help out around the house, above and beyond their regular chores. Others don't. But for extra special help, you may consider some sort of payment; whether that's cash or a family outing is your call. But make your child feel special for the extra effort.

- Start a college savings account and show your child how you contribute toward it and how much it grows each year. Currently, 529 plans are federal and state tax-free, and they're the best thing going these days for college savings.

- You may also want to look into programs like Upromise .com and BabyMint.com, which make contributions to a designated 529 plan for every dollar you spend with an affiliated company (think frequent flier miles, but instead it's frequent shopper dollars). Your child can learn about making decisions such as whether it pays to spend extra money just to get the miles or the dollars into the 529 account (generally, it doesn't).

- Divide birthday and holiday money into three piles: spend it now, short-term savings, and long-term savings (perhaps for college or a car). Encourage them to save: One woman I know doubles all the cash her children put into their bank accounts. But if they withdraw anything before they start college, she gets half. By the time they get to college, she's hoping that the lesson will have sunk in. This same woman also keeps a running tab on the refrigerator of how much her children have in their "pots" at all times, inviting a little friendly competition among the kids about who can be the best saver.

- Give meaningful gifts to your children and nieces, nephews and grandchildren, like shares of stock they'll hold on to instead of a check they'll spend right away.
- Teach your children generosity. Remind them that there are many families far worse off in this world. Being financially savvy means learning how to be happy with what you have (even while you may want more).

Of course, there's no guarantee that all of this will sink in. But you've got a better chance of raising financially aware children if you teach by example.

SIMPLE STEP
35

TALK TO YOUR CHILDREN
OR YOUR HEIRS ABOUT YOUR MONEY

When are your children old enough to know what you have and what you owe? There should come a point in time when you are honest with them about the true state of your finances, for richer or poorer.

After my father died, my mother sat us down and informed us that she wasn't planning on buying a life insurance policy for herself. What we have, she said, will have to do. I had just started college and don't remember that being a particularly scary thought. Within a year my mother had started what would become a highly successful career as a real estate agent, a field in which she earned more than my father ever did in his law practice. And while she worried about being able to "do it all," it was clear to my sisters and me that we didn't have to worry about whether there would be food on the table.

Other parents have a don't-ask, don't-tell rule that keeps their children (who sometimes become their caregiver) in the dark about their money. Financial matters are never discussed, and grown children have no idea whether their parents will die with money in the bank or thousands in debt.

As parents, we're afraid that our children will disclose the status of our wealth to individuals outside the family. Some are afraid that if our children know we have money, they'll do anything to get their hands on it. We have to get over these fears if we want to educate our children about our finances—a task we should face as soon as we feel the kids are ready for the responsibility. If you've raised your children to have ambition and a healthy respect for the power of money and good credit, they will also respect the financial choices and decisions you've made through the years.

But what do you tell children who aren't financially responsible? Who seem oblivious to the financial realities of life? This is a tougher situation, because if your child is a spendthrift, or is into drugs, or makes other foolish personal choices, it could be risky to disclose the status of your wealth. If this is the case, and you still want your child or children to have your money after you're gone, you may be better off working with an estate attorney who can set up a trust that will accomplish your goal of handing out your cash in limited amounts over many years. You can name a responsible friend or family member as the trustee of the account.

Growing up, Robert was his immigrant parents' pride and joy. He was bright, a good student, and responsible. He had an after-school job, always let his parents know where he was, and helped around the house.

But as he entered his teenage years, Robert fell in with the wrong crowd. Sometimes that happens. His grades slipped. He started drinking, and then started using drugs. He would stay out late, which worried his parents to no end, and started missing school. It went from bad to worse. Robert ended up on crack, in and out of jail, and started stealing to support his habit.

Finally, Robert's parents had to shut him down. They refused to give him money and kicked him out of the house. When he begged to come back, they enrolled him in a strict drug rehabilitation program. They, like many parents, are willing to spend what they have to to get him clean and sober, but they won't leave him any cash directly. They understand the battle he'll face the rest of his life to stay sober, and worry that any money they leave him would find its way into a crack house. Someone else in the family will have to dole out money to Robert—if he makes it.

If you have children who are mentally disabled, they may not be able to understand much more than "Mom and Dad will make sure you get everything you need." Physically disabled children may need support as well. If that's the case, there are trusts you can set up that will disburse funds for the continued care of your child that will not interfere with state or federal benefits. Your estate attorney can guide you further.

A GOOD START

When you finally make the decision to sit down with your children, choose a quiet time and a private place for the conversation. Your home or your attorney's office would probably be better than a restaurant, particularly if you have documents, account statements, or other assets you want to show your children.

What should you tell them? Your initial conversation can be the first in a series of talks designed to acquaint your children with what kinds of assets you hold, how they pay out, how much they're worth, and how they should be handled after your death and that of your spouse or partner.

To start, you might hand them a copy of your master account list and important persons contact sheet. With these two items, you can help them see where your accounts and safe deposit box are located (names, addresses, and phone numbers), and who should be contacted in case of an emergency or death.

The next conversation might focus on how much you have in assets, and whether these assets generate income or growth for your portfolio. You can share your reasoning behind the different baskets of investments, and discuss which should be sold first in the event of a catastrophic illness.

Keep the conversations short in length, no more than half an hour, so that your children have an opportunity to absorb the information. If you're planning to leave a substantial amount of your assets to someone else besides your children, or to a nonprofit organization or a museum, talk to your children about why you're doing this.

If you decide to leave your assets to your children or heirs in unequal amounts, take the time to explain this up front to them, so they have an opportunity to ask questions and tell you how they feel. Otherwise, after you're gone, bitterness and rivalry could break out among your children and heirs, causing serious personal rifts that may be difficult to resolve.

Finally, it may happen that you will become disabled or unable to manage your finances for some time before your death. Discuss this possibility with your children, and the likelihood that you may need to give them a power of attorney for health care and financial matters. Explain what these documents will do and how your children or heirs can help. You probably already know which of your children you'll want to give the power of attorney to, but in the conversations about your finances, something may emerge to give you new insight into your children that may change your mind.

SET FINANCIAL RULES BEFORE YOUR CHILDREN GO TO COLLEGE

Sending your child off to college hardly qualifies as a disaster—unless, of course, you've done no planning or saving whatsoever. But what happens on campus could set your child off on a path with significant financial repercussions over the next decade or two.

Many college students head off to school with student loans. The federal government offers several loan programs which allow students to borrow the funds they need for tuition and living expenses and wait until after college or graduate school to begin paying back the government. Parents can also borrow money to assist their children with paying college tuition bills. While the loan payments are steep, many studies have shown that the difference in wages earned by a high school graduate and a college graduate could be more than a million dollars over the course of a lifetime.

Paying back student loans isn't generally the problem. The big problem many college students face is credit card debt. Whether or not students have school loans, a large percentage graduate with as much as $10,000 to $15,000 in credit card debt. Often, these charges grew as the result of spring break or winter holiday vacations, clothes, room or dorm furnishings, or just evenings out with friends.

Many students figure, "I'll just pay it off when I'm out of school working for a living." What they forget is they also have to pay for rent, car loans, utility bills, cell phones, food, clothing, and other items that cost a lot of cash. If they have student loans on top of credit card debt, many college graduates find themselves so deeply mired in debt that they end up in bankruptcy court.

Helping your child understand the relationship between money and what it can buy is one of the most important things you can do as a parent. College is generally the last stop (other than postgraduate work) before real life starts. If your kids don't have a handle on their finances by the time they leave, then a financial disaster certainly awaits.

A GOOD START

Putting your new college student on a strict budget is one way to help teach him or her how to manage funds. Ask your child to write down every cent he or she spends while in college, so that both of you know how much things cost and where the budget is being blown. (Tell your child you won't be mad if he or she has the occasional night out with their friends. That's part of college, too.)

If after a month or so your child's budget is way out of whack with what you can afford to give each month, suggest he or she get a part-time job to help with the expenses. With some searching, it's possible to end up with a job (or several part-time jobs) that not only provides spending money, but gives your child experience that will be valuable when it comes time to look for a "real" job.

(And if not, then at least your kid will know what he or she doesn't want to do for a living!)

Many kids learn about credit cards for the first time when they go off to school—Mom and Dad give them one, or they get one for the campus store. This is typically where they make their first credit card mistakes—ranking pizza parties as "emergencies," charging candy bars and video games along with textbooks, and so on. Walk your child through the first few statements so he or she can see how easy it is to go into credit card debt. Supervise while he or she comes up with a plan to pay off the debt and interest. Don't bail your child out of this important learning experience. Just remember that if you co-sign a credit card for your child and then your child defaults on the account, the credit card company will come after you to pay the bill. And if the bills go unpaid, it's your credit history that will suffer along with that of your child.

The truth is, most college students have time to do something that will contribute to the bottom line. Even premed students can find a lab to work in part-time. Not only will having a real-life work experience help focus your college student, it should help pay the bills. Plenty of students work part-time in labs helping out with experiments, sell blood, assist in meal service, or work at the local newspaper or television station. I worked throughout college. During the year, I wrote for the university newspaper. During the summer, I worked at various retail jobs for the minimum wage plus commission. When I lived abroad my junior year, I worked in a local pub. Senior year, I worked thirty hours a week selling third-party self-insurance plans. My parents always believed in part-time jobs and stressed the importance of contributing to the tuition and room and board bills.

7

Estate Matters

DEVELOP AN ESTATE PLAN

When you're planning for a disaster, it's difficult to get your mind around the idea that you or your loved ones may not be here for the "after" part—as in after you or your spouse or partner pass on.

No one really likes to think about it. But planning what happens to your assets should the unthinkable happen is a central part of making your finances disaster-proof. And so developing an estate plan, in which you make all the big, tough decisions about who is going to get what, is a very important step.

How Much You Have

If you've been working through this book from the beginning, you already have your list of assets. To calculate your net worth (what you have minus what you owe), start by tallying up how much your assets are worth today. Then subtract all of your debts, including car, student, home, and personal loans plus credit card debt.

How much you have is important because it will determine if you need to take any extraordinary measure to limit the amount of tax your estate will have to pay after you die.

Your Net Worth Worksheet

Assets	$	Debts	$
_____	_____	_____	_____
_____	_____	_____	_____
_____	_____	_____	_____
_____	_____	_____	_____
_____	_____	_____	_____
_____	_____	_____	_____
_____	_____	_____	_____
_____	_____	_____	_____
_____	_____	_____	_____

Total _____   Total _____

Assets   _____
Debts   − _____
Net worth = _____

Every dollar your estate doesn't have to pay is another dollar in your pocket (or in the pocket of your loved ones).

If your net worth exceeds $1 million for you and another $1 million for your spouse, you should immediately seek the advice of an estate attorney who can go over options such as trusts that will help you decide how to legally shelter some of your estate. If your estate is valued at less than $1 million (including life insurance and the value of your real estate), then you should be able to pass down most, if not all, of your assets tax-free. (The amount you can pass down tax-free will increase over the years, but it was unclear at tax time whether the final number would be $3 million or $5 million. And, in 2011, these limits may actually shrink.)

And Who Should Get It

This issue is tough enough to eat you up inside. Still, you have to make the time to decide who you would want to have your things after your death. Do you want to leave everything to your spouse or partner? Do you want your assets divided among your spouse or partner, children, and three best friends? Do you want your nieces and nephews to get it? Or do you want to leave it all to charity? Remember, if you don't decide these things now and let other people in your inner circle of family and friends know your wishes, a court could end up deciding who gets what—including control over your children!

A GOOD START

You'll need to find a few different people to fill different jobs on your estate team, including:

An Executor: Gathers assets after your death, oversees the probate proceedings, and distributes assets to your heirs. Anyone of majority age (eighteen or twenty-one in most states) can be an executor, and you can name two or three individuals to be coexecutors. However, it's wise to choose at least one executor who lives in-state.

A Guardian: Raises your minor children if you and your spouse or partner die. (See Simple Step 32.)

A Trustee: Oversees your trust accounts. You can choose a financial institution (like a bank's trust department), but they will charge you fees. A family member may or may not charge a fee for his or her services.

An Agent: An individual you name to make decisions regarding your health care or personal finance in case you can't. (You'll use a durable power of attorney, also known as a power of attorney for health care or power of attorney for financial matters.)

Once you've decided who will handle these duties, your next step is to create an estate plan. An estate planner (a financial planner with special training in handling estates) or estate attorney can help you organize your estate and draft the documentation (typically a will and perhaps a trust) that allows the passing of assets to heirs. Over the next few Simple Steps, I'll discuss the kind of documentation you'll need, including a will, living will, and powers of attorney for health care and financial matters.

Signing Is Everything

You can prepare the most elaborate estate plan, but if you don't sign the paperwork, it's worthless. Be sure to sign all the necessary documents and place them in a safe place. Your attorney should have a copy, and you should keep a copy in your home safe, with the original in your safe deposit box.

Small Business Owners

Will your business carry on after you die? How will that happen? Who will take over? Will there be an income stream after you're gone? Who will receive that money?

When you own a small business, especially a successful one, it's important to find a way to answer these questions, particularly if you have investors or employees. If your business will continue to generate revenue even after you're gone, you'll need to find a way for that income to be received and deposited, for taxes to be paid, and for the cash to be distributed to the right party.

One way to continue a business is to incorporate. A corporation will continue even after the death of the president (you). Another president would then be appointed by the board of directors. But there are other ways to protect your business. Your attorney or tax advisor should be able to suggest a solution for you, particularly if this income is to help support your family after you're gone.

If your business has intrinsic value without you, it will be considered part of your estate for tax purposes. To avoid paying tax on a business that's essentially worthless without you, you'll need to structure the business accordingly. It would be unfortunate for the IRS to value your business at $1 million, for example, when you'd never be able to give it away.

WRITE A WILL AND SIGN IT

A valid, enforceable will could be one of your most important documents. If you sign it and have it properly witnessed and notarized, your estate will be distributed the way you want. If you don't have a will, the state will decide who gets what, and everything (including your children) could be left to the wrong person.

In some states the relative who is legally closest to the deceased (a sister is considered closer than a niece or nephew, for example) will inherit everything. In others, your spouse will get a third and your children will get two-thirds of your estate. You've worked too hard building up your estate to allow probate court to make this final choice for you. If you're not married, and you either die *intestate* (without a will) or you fail to provide for your partner in your will, your partner may be left bereft emotionally *and* financially.

A will doesn't have to be long and complicated, especially if you've taken the time to organize an effective estate plan. On the other hand, you want to make sure your bases are covered. Estate attorneys can draw up a will that is legally binding in the state in which you live. (Be careful if you have two homes, because the government will assume your primary residence is where you spend most of the year and do things like vote. That could pose a tax problem if you die in the state where you have your second home.)

Contesting Wills

It's tough to please everyone, and there may be someone who decides, for whatever reason, to contest your will. Unhappy heirs or would-be heirs can cause a whole lot of problems after you're gone. If you're concerned that someone may fight over what they believe they were entitled to inherit, you should add a no-contest provision to your will. This basically says: If you contest the will, you forfeit your entire bequest. But it won't work to dissuade someone not named in the will from contesting it. (In fact, no-contest provisions are fairly common.)

Another way to protect yourself is to put all of your assets into a revocable trust, also known as a living trust. I'll talk more about that in Simple Step 42.

A GOOD START

You can buy a simple will from a Web site called Nolo.com. Nolo Press publishes many excellent legal books. The site also sells legal documents and legal software. Quicken sells Quicken Lawyer and there are several other legal software choices available at your local office supply company. You can also buy a will from your local stationery store. I like to call these "wills in a box" because they're an all-in-one form that's designed to suit the general masses.

It's tempting to buy a pre-made will, trust, power of attorney, or other legal document, but I urge you to seek the advice of an estate attorney instead. If you want to save some money, you can buy one of these, go through it to know what you want and how you want the document to distribute your assets, and then ask the attorney to modify it to suit your needs. Make sure that the document is legal in your state.

The preparation of a simple will should cost between $400 and $1,000, though I'm sure that cost will drift up over time. Before you decide you can't afford it, remember: If you don't have a will, the state will decide who gets what you have.

Find an estate attorney by asking friends and relatives (especially older or wealthier ones) for a referral. Then call the attorney and discuss what you need. Ask what the fee will be. If you don't have anyone who can give you a referral, you can call the local bar association and ask for a list of names of estate attorneys.

Once you've completed your will, sign and notarize it immediately. It's not valid until you do so.

Name a Guardian

A will is the place to state who should be given guardianship over your minor children. Writing a signed, sealed letter won't do, and while the court may consider it when deciding on placement, there's no obligation to follow your instructions. But if you have a properly executed will, which is a legal document, the court must follow your wishes.

Update as Necessary

If you've already made a will, good for you. Keep it current; it needs to reflect every major financial change: additional children, a second home, and changes in beneficiaries, among other matters.

SIGN A LIVING WILL

A living will tells the world how you want to die, just in case you can't. If you're in a horrible accident, you could have signed a statement that basically says you do not want any measures taken that will prolong your life unnecessarily. On the other hand, if you don't sign a living will, doctors are obligated by law to do everything they can to sustain and prolong your life.

Here's the central passage of a living will:

> If at any time I should have an incurable and irreversible injury, disease, or illness judged to be a terminal condition by my attending physician who has personally examined me and has determined that my death is imminent except for death-delaying procedures and has verified that determination in writing, I direct that such procedures which would only pro-long the dying process be withheld or withdrawn and that I be permitted to die naturally with only the administration of med-ication, sustenance, or the performance of any medical proce-dure deemed necessary by my attending physician, to provide me with comfort care.

Any way you cut it, signing a living will is a difficult thing to do. You're declaring your mortality to the world and tying up the loose ends. However difficult it is for you to sign the living will, it's minor compared to the rough time your family members and friends will have in the hospital if you're hooked up to a dozen machines that are keeping you alive, and a fight breaks out over what you'd really want them to do.

Knowing what your wishes are can save the people closest to you from an emotional dispute that could tear apart your entire family, not to mention deplete your loved ones' savings accounts.

A GOOD START

You can buy a living will in a stationery store, or from a Web site like Nolo.com. You can even go to a local library and copy the statute from the state court books (ask the librarian for help). It may even be available through your state's Web site.

Once you have your living will, you must sign and date it. Then you must have it signed by as many witnesses as your state requires. Many states require three witnesses. If the living will isn't properly signed, it will be considered invalid. Have your living will checked over by an attorney.

No matter what your living will says, if no one knows of the document's existence, it won't matter. So if you want your living will to be effective, share it with your doctor, close family members, attorney, spouse, and best friends.

SIGN A
POWER OF ATTORNEY
FOR HEALTH CARE

A power of attorney, also known as a *durable power of attorney*, is a document that gives someone the right to act on your behalf. A power of attorney for health care gives your designated agent the right to make decisions about your health care in the event you are unable to do so.

Technically, you should sign both a living will and a power of attorney for health care, although there is some overlap. If you don't have a living will, but have signed a power of attorney for health care, your designated agent can tell the doctors what your final wishes would be in terms of life-prolonging medical care.

But it doesn't work the other way. Let's assume you develop a disease like Alzheimer's, which robs you of your mind. Your body is relatively healthy physically, but you are deemed incompetent to make decisions for yourself. In this case a living will is useless. A power of attorney for health care gives your designated agent the right to make medical decisions, including putting you in a hospital, nursing home, or other institution, or giving you the medical attention you need. Your agent can authorize medical attention on your behalf.

A GOOD START

Choosing the person who will make these important decisions about your health care might be difficult. Look first to your spouse or partner, then your children, and then your other relatives, to see if there is someone who is strong enough to accept the responsibility of implementing your final wishes with respect to medical attention. And don't forget to ask that individual if he or she is willing to take this on. Being a designated agent for health care could mean stepping into the middle of a huge family fight, particularly if some family members hold strong religious beliefs. You won't do yourself or anyone else any favors if you choose someone who is not up to the task.

Finally, make sure your designated agent for health care decisions has a copy of your properly executed living will. That will give you a much better chance of having your wishes followed in an emergency.

SIGN A DURABLE POWER OF ATTORNEY FOR FINANCIAL MATTERS

A durable power of attorney for financial matters, also known in some states as a *durable power of attorney for property*, is one of the most powerful legal documents. It gives your designated agent the ability to pledge, sell, or otherwise dispose of your real estate or other personal property without giving you advance notice or seeking your approval. Unless you limit the term of the document, your agent can continue to represent you indefinitely.

While your designated agent is supposed to represent your best interests, you can easily see how choosing the wrong person could mean you'd wind up broke (or worse!). You can end a power of attorney by revoking the grant of power. This can be done with or without the agent's knowledge.

There are different times in life when you may sign a power of attorney. If you're buying or selling a home and can't attend the closing, for example, you can sign a power of attorney and have either your attorney or another designated agent sign the documents on your behalf.

When you're preparing an estate plan, the power of attorney for financial matters gives someone the right to pay bills, sell assets, and invest your money whether you're able to do so or not. If you choose your agent wisely, he or she may be able to slowly sell off pieces of your estate to pay for special or experimental medical treatments or a nursing home—costs that may not be covered by your insurance policy.

A GOOD START

You probably don't think you need a power of attorney for financial matters because you can't ever imagine yourself incapable of writing a check to the cable company. And you don't want to hand someone the right to make financial decisions for you when you're perfectly healthy.

Which you are today—but might not be tomorrow.

If you have concerns about signing a power of attorney for financial matters, talk with your attorney about ways in which you can limit the term of the document. Perhaps you'll sign a new one every year. Perhaps your document will go into effect only if your physician judges you to be mentally incompetent. Your attorney should certainly be able to come up with some language that will ease your mind.

You may want to choose someone other than the agent you've designated as your power of attorney for health care. Why? First, you may not want to place the burden of dealing with your health issues and financial issues on the same individual. If you're seriously ill, you'll want one person at the hospital monitoring your medical treatment. That person (who will doubtless have his or her own busy life) may not have the time or mental capacity to work on keeping your financial life moving full steam ahead simultaneously. Second, the person you choose to monitor your health issues may not be as financially savvy as you'd like.

You'll want to choose someone as your power of attorney for financial matters who either has your money values or respects how you've handled your investments.

Whomever you choose, be sure to ask first before giving him or her power of attorney. Plan to take the time to sit down with your designated agent and walk him or her through your assets and what you think should be done with them when the time comes.

CONSIDER PUTTING YOUR ASSETS INTO A LIVING TRUST

There are two kinds of trusts: *revocable* and *irrevocable*. An irrevocable trust means you give away direct control over your assets permanently. Once an irrevocable trust is set up, it can't be changed or altered. And because you are, in effect, giving away your assets permanently, there currently may be estate tax benefits to setting up an irrevocable trust.

A revocable trust, also known as a *living trust*, allows you to transfer your stocks, property, and other assets into the trust. For as long as you live, you are the trust's beneficiary. You can change or modify the trust as frequently as time and dollars permit.

There are a couple of benefits to a living trust. First, it allows you to do exactly what a will does, including designate who will be the trust's beneficiary after you die. It also permits a speedy transfer of assets. You'll save something on your probate filing fees (since in some states probate may not even be necessary if you have a living trust). And it helps straighten things out if you own assets in several states (including homes or investment property, businesses, or boats).

Living trusts are often referred to by different names. The key to decoding these goofy names (like "sweetheart trust") is to see whether they're revocable. If you can revoke the trust, it's a living trust—no matter what it's called. (Often people are confused why you'd need a living trust *and* a will. If you have only a will, your estate will likely have to go through probate court, a process where the court affirms ownership of your assets and approves their disposition to your heirs. If you have a living trust in addition to a will, the trust has already taken care of the ownership and disposition issues, so you may be able to bypass probate. Why bypass probate? Depending on the complexity of assets, and the state in which you live, probate can be an expensive and time-consuming process for your heirs.)

A GOOD START

The problem with all trusts is that they're worthless unless you actually take the time to transfer assets into them. With a living trust, you can have a sentence written into your will that will effectively transfer all of your assets into your trust at the time of death. Or you can take the time to transfer the deed to your home, for example, from your name into your living trust with you as beneficiary. (By the way, you might pay a filing fee to transfer the deed, but since you're not selling your home, you shouldn't or may not have to pay transfer taxes. Check with your attorney for details on what is required in your state.)

The nicest thing about trusts is that ownership transfers automatically upon your death. It's like naming beneficiaries of your life insurance policy or 401(k). But you need to make sure the beneficiaries of your trust are updated to reflect your changing life. For example, if you get divorced and remarried, you should change the name of the contingent beneficiary from your ex-spouse to your current spouse. If you have children, you may wish to name them as beneficiaries. You will be able to designate what percentage of the trust will go to each contingent beneficiary.

The cost to draft a simple living trust ranges from $500 to $2,000. Again, if you don't take the time to transfer assets into the trust, you've just wasted your money.

(With the estate tax in flux, you may not wish to sign an irrevocable trust, since the document would survive even if the estate tax disappears entirely. If you need some protection from estate taxes, talk to your estate attorney about what short-term (say, two to ten years) options may be available to you.)

MAKE YOUR FUNERAL PLANS

When former Beatle George Harrison died, he asked that he be cremated and his ashes thrown into the Ganges River. He wanted his final resting place to be a place that moved him spiritually.

Planning your funeral, and taking care of the expenses up front, is the final part of your estate plan. Where you'd like to be buried or cremated, what kind of service would be meaningful to you, and who should participate, are all decisions you can make today that will ease the financial and emotional burden on your loved ones after you're gone.

Jeanne and Meyer lived until they were in their late nineties. They were fairly healthy physically and all there mentally, right up until the end. Because they lived so much longer than they had ever dreamed, Meyer decided to make all of their funeral arrangements ahead of time. He paid in full for their graves, funerals, caskets, flowers, service, and even perpetual care for the gravesites. Then, he and Jeanne labeled all of the objects in their apartment, so there would be no fighting among their nieces and nephews. Once they'd taken care of their funeral arrangements and the bequeathing of their keepsakes, they could relax and enjoy the rest of their lives.

Of course, making your final arrangements is difficult to do emotionally and you may find yourself repulsed by the idea of picking out your own grave, headstone, plot, service, and funeral company.

If you're religious (no matter which religion you belong to), some of these choices will be easier. In some religions cremation isn't permitted. In others it's common. Typically, each religion prescribes a formal ceremony. But if you don't subscribe to any one religious faith, all the possibilities are open.

A GOOD START

Start by deciding where you'd like your final resting place to be. Will it be a cemetery close by or one that's convenient for friends and family to visit? Will you be cremated, with your ashes in an urn, or will you ask that they be spread in a certain location?

If you decide you want to be in a specific cemetery, you'll want to call and make an appointment to see what gravesites are available. Decide how many graves you'll want or need. When my grandmother died thirty years ago, my grandfather bought six plots in the same cemetery where my grandmother's family was buried. He planned for my grandmother and himself, my mother and father, and my uncle and aunt. Unfortunately, two untimely deaths and a remarriage left the plot one grave too short. Another one of life's curve balls.

Once you've negotiated with the cemetery and paid for your plots, you're stuck with that plan unless you're willing to walk away from a substantial investment. The secondary market for funeral plots just isn't that strong. So take care in making your decision.

When it comes to buying coffins and having a funeral, you can spend hundreds of dollars or tens of thousands. Don't let anyone talk you into a more expensive funeral package than you really want—or can afford. Choose a funeral home that has been in business for a long time and has a good reputation. You won't want to pay up front for your funeral, only to have the funeral home go out of business the day before you need it.

Finally, decide what type of service you want. Open or closed casket? Religious or memorial service (or both, if that's appropriate)? Who will conduct and participate in the service? I knew a woman who decided not only who should participate, but what they should read and in what order. It's your funeral, as they say, your final opportunity to choreograph the moment.

Once you've decided what you want, and have made the arrangements, sit down and discuss your plans with your family. It's important they understand your wants and feelings now, while they can raise any objections or make suggestions.

Danny was diagnosed with pancreatic cancer and was told he had only a few days, or maybe a week, to live. He decided to have an open casket at his wake, in keeping with his religious beliefs. Unfortunately, he didn't share his plans with everyone. After he had died, one daughter objected to having an open casket and caused a family fight at a very difficult time. The casket ultimately stayed open, but there were some bad feelings all around.

Organ Donation

Your final plans may include donating your organs or donating your body to science. Every state has an organ donor card you can sign that legalizes the immediate transfer of your organs once you've died. In many states, you simply sign the back of your driver's license. But again, if you don't have your driver's license with you and you haven't told your agent who has the power of attorney for health care, your wishes may not be followed.

Tell your family, your friends, and your loved ones if you plan to be an organ donor. Some of those closest to you may be uncomfortable with the notion. Better to find out now than later, when every second counts.

If you're interested in leaving your body to science, you can call your closest major university's science department or medical school to see if they have any need for human cadavers. The university or medical school will tell you how to proceed and should furnish you any documentation you need.

Help for Planning a Funeral

A quick Internet search turned up more than 3 million pages with the word "funeral" in them. The following sites, however, appear to offer some information of value for consumers. Use them to give yourself an idea of different options and costs that may be available to you when making your arrangements. You'll also find good information about elder-care and hospices.

National Funeral Director's Association
NFDA.org.

This nonprofit association offers consumers guidelines on preneed contracts ("preneed" means before you actually need the services), plus tips for successfully negotiating funeral arrangements and contracts.

The Funeral Services Information Portal and Directory
Thefuneraldirectory.com

This site offers searchable consumer and business directories plus information on how you can arrange or preplan a funeral, write a eulogy, survivor benefits, wills, living wills, home care, and other topics.

Funeral Consumers Alliance
Funerals.org

A nonprofit funeral industry watchdog group that includes consumer warnings about specific organizations. Check here before you sign to make sure you're not getting ripped off.

Funeral Ethics Association
2115 South Grand Avenue West
Springfield, Illinois 62704
(217) 525-1520
Fea.org

This nonprofit association offers free mediation services between consumers and funeral service providers. The Web site offers explanations of common consumer complaints and issues.

Funeral Help Program
Dragonet.com/funeral/about.htm

The information on this site comes from the book *The Affordable Funeral: Going in Style, Not in Debt,* by Dr. R. E. Markin. At press time, he was also the director of the Alzheimer's Research Foundation, which sponsors the site. The book is available online, through your local bookseller, or at your local public library.

Military Funeral Honors Homepage
Militaryfuneralhonors.osd.mil

This page is sponsored by the U.S. government and provides information on who is eligible for military funeral honors, what services are provided, funeral directors that can help with a military burial, and other related links.

8

After the Disaster

SIMPLE STEP
44

DON'T BE AFRAID TO ASK FOR HELP

Everyone reacts to life's curve balls in a different way. Some forge ahead with barely a pause, and break down later after the crisis subsides. Others go to bed and don't rise to rejoin the world for days, weeks, or even months. Most of us take it day by day until we can reweave the fabric of our lives and move on.

In the days after a disaster, you can expect life to turn upside down. Things that made sense before may not now. Depending on what kind of disaster struck, you may be feeling sad, lost, confused, angry, and completely out of sorts, a phenomenon known as "post-traumatic stress disorder," which is one way our bodies and minds cope with the unimaginable.

Losing one child qualifies as a disaster. But imagine losing six of your nine children all at once. That's what happened to one family, whose minivan was hit by a truck driver. After years in court, and a large insurance settlement, the family has moved on. But in the immediate aftermath, there was chaos: planning for six funerals while coping with a media circus and a state investigation. It is almost unimaginable.

Still, life continues even after disaster and we must find a way to get the bills paid, put food on the table, clean and clothe ourselves and our children, and do what needs to be done.

If you're struggling to cope with all of this after losing a spouse, partner, your business, or your job, don't do it alone. Enlist your friends and family. Ask for help in getting your life or business up and running again. Or if that seems like too much, accept the help that is being offered by those around you.

Food is an easy offering to accept. After a death, family and friends will often bring over a casserole or order in dinner for you. Eventually you'll want to eat something. Asking someone to help you sort out and pay your bills is tougher, but that, too, must be done. If you have an attorney in the family, ask for help in gathering together the necessary paperwork.

Your friends and family can help you through a difficult time, but you have to let them. For some folks, the psychological need to be in control of every facet of our existence is the toughest barrier to overcome.

Small Business Owners

If you lose your place of business in a fire, flood, tornado, hurricane, or terrorist attack, you need to try to figure out a way to get your business up and running again as soon as possible. Don't let any obstacle, including loss of data, computers, papers, telephones, ledgers, or even staff, stop you from trying.

Vladimir was an entrepreneur. He did everything from driving a taxicab to working in the building trades. His last effort was as a furrier. He started a small business selling sheepskin and leather coats out of his house and car. Then he rented a small store in a mall not too far from where he lived and sold his wares there.

The coats were beautiful, and the store started to prosper. But, suddenly, Vladimir died. When his son went into the store to see what was going on, everything was in turmoil. It turned out that most of the business was in Vladimir's head—that is, he didn't have many written records of what was sold, or what was in inventory, or what was owed to the suppliers. Fortunately, another relative, who was retired, stepped in and spent more than six weeks doing inventory, calling suppliers, and cataloging whatever records the store had. Then they held a large going-out-of-business sale.

While all this was going on, of course, Vladimir's family had to plan for his funeral and cope with the loss of a wonderful husband and father.

Sometimes businesses die in a disaster because paying clients disappear. That happened to one computer consultant in the aftermath of a hurricane. His business evaporated because all of his clients went out of business. But if you don't try, you'll never know if you could have succeeded simply by getting back in the saddle as soon as possible.

If you're a small business owner struggling with the loss of a partner, or the survivor/inheritor of a small business, there may be low-cost resources available to you that will help you keep the business going long enough to either end it profitably or take over. Check out the Small Business Administration (sba.gov) for resources and to apply for low-cost loans.

A GOOD START

Make a list of all the things, large and small, that need to be done. Use the worksheet below to help jog your memory and add to it as necessary. Next to each task, write down the name of someone who can help you do this job for the next month or two (after the disaster). I'm not suggesting that you won't need help later down the line, but right now you're just trying to meet your immediate needs. Ask these people if they would be kind enough to help you do certain things for the first few months, until you're back on your feet and thinking clearly again.

Immediate Needs Worksheet

Job   **Family Member/Friend**

Grocery store/pharmacy   _____

Cook or order meals   _____

Pay mortgage and other bills/
   enter into computer   _____

Work on budget   _____

Arrange funeral/medical needs   _____

Wash clothes/arrange for dry
   cleaners   _____

Carpool kids/take to school   _____

Clean house/arrange for cleaning
   service   _____

Babysitter/entertainment for kids   _____

Legal issues/gathering documents   _____

Tax issues/filing income taxes   _____

Insurance issues/calling insurers   _____

Bank issues/credit card issues   _____

Finding a financial planner   _____

Organizing notes/writing
   thank-you notes   _____

Car repairs   _____

Other   _____

Other   _____

Other   _____

Other   _____

Other   _____

Other   _____

If you feel you'll be putting people out if you ask them for help, get over it. Instead, think of how you'd feel if one of your friends or family members were in the same situation and asked *you* for help. You'd probably feel grateful that they thought enough of your relationship to ask, and would be honored to help them out in this time of crisis. And that's how those closest to you will feel. They'll want to do something to help. What you're doing is giving them a constructive way to help in a way that's most meaningful to you.

GATHER YOUR
IMPORTANT DOCUMENTS

In times of crisis, organization puts you way ahead of the game. Not only will it ease some of your anxiety (because you'll know what you have, where it is, and how to access it), but you will be able to move more quickly to collect insurance proceeds and work out any settlements that are owed.

What you'll need to do now is collect your important documents and construct a plan for getting any additional documentation you'll need to move forward. These will vary, depending on the type of crisis (for example, job loss versus death). But use the worksheet to check off each document as you gather it and put it in one place.

Depending on what's happened, you may need to get certified copies of a death certificate. These are typically available at your local county offices. There is a small fee for each copy ordered, but without it you will not be able to prove legally that someone has died.

In the case of a long-term illness, you may need to start a file in which you keep all medical records and bills that you receive. Keep these in a separate folder, but in the same general place as all of your other important records.

A GOOD START

Use this worksheet to make sure you have all of your important documents together in one place. If you're having trouble getting some of the documents, ask a family member or friend to assist you.

Important Documents Worksheet

Document	Have It?
Birth certificate(s)	_____
Death certificate(s)	_____
Medical bills	_____
Insurance policies	_____
Life	_____
Auto	_____
Health	_____
Disability	_____
Long-term care	_____
Umbrella	_____
Homeowners	_____
Flood	_____
Earthquake	_____
Other	_____
Estate documents	_____
Will	_____
Living will	_____
Power of attorney for health care	_____
Power of attorney for financial matters	
Trust(s)	_____
Bank account statements	_____
Retirement account statements	_____
Most recent tax return	_____
Copy of titles to property owned	_____
Real estate	_____
Car(s)	_____
Boat(s)	_____
Plane(s)	_____
Other	_____

Copies of stocks/bonds
  not held in street name
  (brokerage firm)   _____

Loan documents/statements   _____

Warranties for big-ticket items   _____

Home purchase/sale and capital
  improvement records   _____

Copy of credit cards/statements   _____

Copy of investment statements   _____

Other investment information   _____

Copy of driver's license or
  state ID card   _____

Passport   _____

Visa or green card   _____

Marriage certificate,
  divorce decree, judgments, etc.   _____

Child adoption/custody agreement   _____

Birth certificate(s) for children   _____

Funeral arrangement
  documentation   _____

Passport(s)   _____

Social Security card(s)   _____

START MAKING YOUR CALLS

One thing about personal financial crises, there's a lot of phone calling and paperwork involved. You'll need to inform your friends and family. Then you'll need to call your attorney and perhaps your tax advisor. Finally, you'll need to inform companies about the crisis, find out what documentation they need, and perhaps change names on numerous accounts. It's time-consuming and can be mind-numbing. And it's easy to procrastinate, even if you could really use the insurance proceeds.

At some point after a serious accident, death, fire, flood, disability, or job loss, you'll need to pick up the telephone. If you just can't face making calls to insurance companies, banks, lenders, or the hospital, then ask someone close to you to help make some of those calls. At this time, having your contact list handy will help enormously.

Insurance Companies

After an accident, death, or disability, one of the first things you should do is look at your policies to see if you're enti-tled to proceeds, and if so, how much. But many people put this further down on the list, delaying the initial call. And I suppose if money is no object, you can wait a few extra days or weeks to contact your insurance company. But for most of us getting a check in hand takes time, and during that time your liquid cash can dry up fairly quickly.

The longer you wait to make the initial call, the longer it will be before you receive a payout from your insurance company. You may need to provide your insurance company with different sorts of paperwork in order to prove your claim, from a death certificate to a police report to medical bills. Life, business, and disability insurance checks can take weeks to process.

Banks and Investment Firms

If your spouse or partner has died, you may need to change the names on your accounts, including checking, savings, money market, CDs, and brokerage accounts. Stocks or bonds that are held jointly, in street name (that is, by the brokerage firm instead of by you), will need to be changed to reflect the new owners. Retirement and other accounts that only have your spouse or partner's name on them may be frozen by the financial institution until you can prove who is the rightful heir of the account.

If you find yourself really tight on cash, take steps immediately to lessen the burden so you don't end up ruining your credit and perhaps even losing your home. If you have a mortgage on your property, lenders will often help you through a difficult time, either by refinancing your home loan (if rates are lower, and if you have the income to qualify for the new loan), or by allowing you to pay only the interest on your loan (and extending the time of your loan repayment by three or six months). There are several ways lenders can help. Talk to your lender's "loss mitigation" department for more information.

If you're over the age of sixty-two, and your home is mortgage-free (or virtually mortgage-free), but you're still having trouble scraping together enough cash to pay your bills, you may want to investigate a reverse mortgage. A reverse mortgage will allow you to receive either a small payment each month, or a lump sum. The total amount will equal about half of your home's value, but you will not have to pay back this amount until the home is sold.

There are two Web sites that fully explain reverse mortgages: Reverse.org (which is run by the guy who helped invent reverse mortgages) and Homepath.com (the consumer Web site run by Fannie Mae, the nation's largest secondary market lender).

Real Property

After a death you may need to change the title to any real property owned, including a home, second home, boat, plane, or artwork. You may need (but may not be required) to call your lender regarding changing the names on your home loan as well (changing the name on the property deed is a title issue, not a loan issue). Some of this may happen during the probate process. If the properties are in a trust, the ownership will change automatically upon the owner's death.

Small Business Owners

Should your business be destroyed, you'll call your insurance agent to find out where you stand with your business interruption insurance. Your agent should put you in touch with an adjuster who can help you through the claims process.

A GOOD START

Open your important documents file and pull out your asset contacts list. Start with your attorney and work your way down. When it comes to dealing with insurance companies and financial institutions, call their toll-free number (you'll find it on the policy or brochure if it isn't already in your contacts list) to start the process of changing names and filing claims.

Be prepared to spend some time on the phone with each company, and have a pad and a pen nearby to take notes on what each company requires to file the claim or make a name change on an account. Always get the agent's name, ID number, call reference number, and phone number, and jot down the time and date you spoke in order to create the all-important paper trail (just in case something goes wrong—which it already has).

Once you've created the master list of who needs what, assemble the required copies of documentation and work your way down the list, noting the date you got the paperwork and keeping copies of any cover letters for your records.

DON'T MAKE IMMEDIATE
FINANCIAL DECISIONS WITH
LONG-TERM CONSEQUENCES

When a financial crisis hits, our first impulse is to make a drastic change. We may feel we're doing it for financial reasons, but there's usually a strong emotional component as well. After a job loss or death, you might feel an urge to sell your home and move to get away from it all. Or you may want to sell stocks and bonds to have ready cash. Or invest in the stock market with insurance proceeds in the hope of building up a quick nest egg.

But emotional instability goes hand in hand with a personal crisis. So making immediate decisions that could have long-term financial consequences isn't usually a good idea. You're taking a huge risk that your judgment will be impaired, and you'll wind up making a poor choice. A second financial fallout could be right behind this one.

Allow some time to pass before making a major decision. You're probably fine when it comes to deciding whether to eat out or order in on a given night. On the other hand, try to wait at least a year before deciding whether you're going to sell your home, move to another state, and start another life. After a year, your inclination to flee might have died down, but if you've already acted on it and sold your home, you won't be able to move back in.

When Pam lost her husband and two daughters in that tragic boating accident, her initial impulse was to pick up her son, George, and flee her houseful of memories. A year later, she decided to renovate instead of move. Slowly, room by room, she remodeled, repainted, and packed away the clothing, toys, and paintings—memories of a lifetime.

Not only has Pam turned her home into a showplace, she has also made it a happy house again, one that she and George can share for as long as they care to stay. It also turned out to be a good investment, as the house has continued to appreciate and is worth much more today because of her improvements.

It's also a good idea to wait to make anything other than a conservative investment. Instead of investing in individual stocks or bonds, you may want to invest your money in a broad, index-based mutual fund, like an S&P 500 (Standard & Poor's top 500 companies in America) fund, or a total market fund. You can buy a short-term bond fund, which will hold thousands of individual bonds and give you a diversified base. Finally, you can keep cash rolling over in a short-term certificate of deposit (CD) or in a money market account, which will allow you enough liquidity to pay your bills, but will earn more money than a regular checking account.

A GOOD START

It's important to identify what your financial impulse is: Are you thinking of buying, selling, moving, quitting your job, taking a job, or traveling? Whichever move you want to make, think about what would happen if you waited until a year from now.

Try to keep your options open:

- Instead of moving across the country, consider renting an apartment for a few weeks or a month in the area in which you're interested to see if you'll like it there before you commit to selling your home and moving your life.

- Instead of selling your home, consider redecorating to make it a "happy" house in the aftermath of a crisis. For a relatively small amount of money, you can repaint and recarpet your home, giving it a whole new feel.

- Instead of investing your cash quickly in an investment you may not understand, put your money into short-term CDs, so that it's relatively liquid but still earning something.

- Instead of blowing your insurance proceeds on a new car, house, or trip around the world, spend time working through the numbers with a financial planner, so you'll know how much cash you'll need to live on.

A year might seem to be a long time after a crisis hits. But in reality once you start feeling better, time begins to fly again. At the first anniversary of the crisis, you can reassess your situation and decide if now is the time to make your big financial move.

SPEND A FEW HOURS WITH A FEE-ONLY FINANCIAL PLANNER

Feeling secure about your finances gives you the intellectual space to focus on your emotional recovery after a crisis. But unless you're Microsoft founder Bill Gates (or have wealth somewhat close to his), it may be difficult to feel safe enough.

The uncertainty can come from not understanding the true picture of your financial future and how your recent crisis may have altered your plans. Although consumers are quite able to crunch the numbers using a wide variety of calculators available for free on various Web sites, it's comforting to have someone you trust look over your information and tell you "Everything is going to be all right."

Hiring a fee-only financial planner can be a good first step toward gaining confidence in your financial future. The financial planner can help walk you through your short-term and long-term expenses and how you'll manage to cope with them. He or she can also draft a new financial and estate plan that meets your changing needs.

The problem with being emotionally caught up in your own personal crisis is that it's sometimes difficult to hear (and understand) what the planner is saying. So make sure you bring a notepad and pen to your appointment. Ask the planner to write out his or her suggestions so you'll be able to take them home and think about them in the quiet and privacy of your own home.

A GOOD START

There are different sorts of financial professionals. A *registered investment advisor* (RIA) typically takes on clients with a greater net worth and charges them a percentage of total assets to do their investing for them. It wouldn't be atypical to pay a registered investment advisor 1 to 2 percent of your total net worth per year. Hopefully, the advisor is generating enough of a return on your portfolio to make the fee you'll pay worthwhile. Be sure to ask a registered investment advisor for parts I and II of their ADV (advisor's) form that they must file with securities regulators. You can find out more from the **National Association of Securities Dealers** (NASD) public disclosure hotline (800-289-9999).

A *certified financial planner* (CFP) can either be fee-only, in which you're charged hourly or by the project for their advice, or conventional, in which you'll be charged a commission and/or a percentage of your assets in exchange for the management of your portfolio and advice. A financial planner will likely be licensed to sell you all sorts of stuff, including insurance and mutual funds, many of which may have a front- or back-end load (sales commission). If a financial planner charges you this way, you may pay a lot for not that much. You can also check on your financial planner's (and stockbroker's, for that matter) background by contacting the NASD's public disclosure hotline.

A fee-only financial planner should charge you either hourly or a set fee for whatever project you ask him or her to take on. For example, if you ask a fee-only financial planner to help you map out your financial future, you can expect to pay up to $200 per hour for his or her services. You can find a fee-only financial planner by calling the **National Association of Personal Financial Advisors** toll-free (888-FEE-ONLY). You can also try the **Financial Planning Association** (800-282-PLAN). Once a year some of the financial magazines rate the top financial advisors in the country. You might look there for a referral to an advisor near you (or if they're too far, call their office and ask for a referral that's closer to where you live). You should also ask the planner to send you a copy of parts I and II of his ADV.

Another option is to use a *certified public accountant* (CPA) who is also a *personal financial specialist* (PFS). This way, you get tax advice mixed in with your financial advice. Contact the **American Institute of Certified Public Accountants** (888-777-7077) or online at CPAPSF.org.

If you're having trouble finding an appropriate financial advisor, you may want to try the big investment firms. Many investment houses, like Fidelity Investments, Charles Schwab, and Merrill Lynch, recognize that many people of moderate means (as opposed to clients with a high net worth) need financial planning advice. These companies have always offered stock brokerage services, but are now expanding their areas of expertise to include basic financial planning. Be sure that you get what you pay for. Many of these companies will charge $250 to $500 (less if you have substantial assets that you may end up depositing with them) for a full financial plan that examines what you have, what you owe, what you pay each month and makes recommendations that will hopefully improve your net worth.

A word of warning: These firms want your cash and they want you to pay for other services they offer. So don't immediately take the broker's suggestions and buy lots of *front-loaded mutual funds* (you pay a big commission when you put cash into these mutual funds compared with *"no load" mutual funds* that don't charge up-front commissions, are cheaper to own, and typically do just as well). For more information on mutual funds, check out Morningstar.com.

Try to get up to five names of different financial planners in your area. Do your background check (to make sure they have no disciplinary problems) and then call to schedule a preliminary meeting. When you go in for your meeting, the planner should be happy to spend a few minutes with you. Ask to see a financial plan for another client. Ask how much the planner charges per hour and if there is a retainer you can pay that will allow you to call with questions throughout the year. Try to get a sense of whether the planner is listening to your needs and concerns. Does the advice and commentary sound canned or fresh? Do you like and trust this planner enough to talk about your most personal financial information? If not, cross this person off the list.

Assuming the planner sounds good and offers you interesting planning and investment options, ask for a few references. Then call and ask these clients if they enjoyed working with the planner. You have to expect that the financial planner will have given you the numbers of his happiest clients, so ask questions that will make them really think about their experiences:

- Does the planner call you back quickly?
- How often do you call the planner?
- If the planner is investing the client's assets, ask what kind of return the portfolio has generated over the course of the years.
- Ask what the planner's biggest strengths and weaknesses are.

These are all questions you can ask the financial planner as well. Remember, if you don't like and trust the planner, he or she can't do the best job for you. (For more information about investing, check out my book *100 Questions You Should Ask About Your Personal Finances*.)

SIMPLE STEP
49

DON'T TAKE HOT TIPS
FROM A COLD CALL

There are con artists who specialize in funerals. Every day, they peruse the death notices in the local paper to see who died. Then they go to the funeral, pretend to know the dead, chum up with the bereaved, and offer to help them with their finances. What they mean, of course, is to help them empty their wallets and bank accounts.

Other con artists peruse the death notices and show up at the wake and funeral to learn something about the deceased. Then they call the bereaved and tell them that their loved one was about to make an investment. Because the widow or widower's first instinct will be to do whatever the deceased wanted, the investment is often made.

When a crisis happens, it takes your attention away from the mundane tasks of life: paying the bills, feeding your family, even going to work. You're at your most vulnerable because you're using all of your brain power to cope with whatever crisis there is. Scam artists and crooks prey on our vulnerabilities. And then, of course, we get taken.

An easy way to avoid being scammed is to remember these two rules:

1. Never take hot tips from a cold call.
2. If it appears too good to be true, it is.

Never Take Hot Tips from a Cold Call

Let's look at the first rule: How many times has your dinner been interrupted by someone who wanted to sell you something? It could be an extended warranty for an appliance, home siding, an insurance program for your credit card, or even hot stocks. But the caller is sure that he or she has THE deal for you. All you have to do is agree. They'll bill you later.

The truth is, telemarketing firms are rarely pushing something that's a good deal for you. In fact, to be on the safe side, just assume that there's nothing a telemarketer could tell you that you'd want to hear. There's nothing they have to sell that you'd want to buy (If it sounds *that* good, ask them to send you literature and then hang up.). And if a telemarketer has a hot stock tip, be skeptical. If this was such a great deal, why hasn't the telemarketer borrowed every cent he could get his hands on and made himself rich? The answer, of course, is that telemarketers are doing a job, which is to sell you something. Your answer should always be "No thanks."

If It Appears Too Good to Be True, It Is

I wish I had a dollar for every time someone wrote me a letter or called my radio program to tell me about a fantastic deal they stumbled across. These include letters from people in Africa (frequently, it's Nigeria—I don't know why) asking you to let them use your bank account to deposit $10 million and then you keep $1 million or even all $10 million. I got an e-mail from someone in Oman asking me to send them hundreds of copies of my books, and if I also included my bank account routing numbers, they would electronically send me payment. People also believe that they can "wipe" their credit clean, or get a "brand new Social Security number" and start over again.

Balderdash. All of these are verifiable scams that federal agents have uncovered over and over again. No one is going to give you free money for anything. If you give someone you don't know your personal financial information (including Social Security number, driver's license number, name, address, and bank account information), you are essentially offering someone the opportunity to steal your identity and ruin your credit.

So on top of whatever crisis you're dealing with at the moment, you may also become the victim of a financial information crime. While eventually you may get everything straightened out, it can take years and cost you thousands of dollars in legal bills.

Are there real deals out there? Absolutely. But you have to be the one to seek them out. Be suspicious of any so-called "deals" that turn up on your doorstep, particularly if they come when you're in crisis mode and more vulnerable than usual.

A GOOD START

One way to cut down on the number of telemarketers and junk mail is to write to the organizations listed below and request your name be taken off their mailing lists. You'll need to do this about every six months, but it definitely cuts down on the amount of junk mail and telephone calls you'll receive—and cuts down on the number of opportunities to end up buying something you don't want and don't need. Some states, like Georgia and New York, have state do-not-call lists. The Federal Trade Commission (FTC) has proposed a federal do-not-call list as well. Contact your state Consumer Information office for details. You can check my Web site, thinkglink.com, for more information and updates as they become available.

Direct Mail Name Removal

You may register with the name removal file by mailing your name(s) and home address and signature in a letter or on a postcard to:

Mail Preference Service
Direct Marketing Association
P.O. Box 9008
Farmingdale, NY 11735-9008
Web site: www.e-mps.org

Telemarketing Name Removal

You may register with this DO-NOT-CALL file by sending your name(s), home address, and home telephone number (including area code) and signature in a letter or on a postcard to:

Telephone Preference Service
Direct Marketing Association
P.O. Box 9014
Farmingdale, NY 11735-9014

Opting Out

Call (888) 5OPT-OUT to opt out of having credit bureaus sell your personal information, which means you'll receive fewer preapproved credit cards in the mail. You should also contact your financial services companies (banks, investment companies, credit card companies, etc.) and tell them you want to "opt out." You'll fill out a form or give them information over the phone that will remove your name from telemarketing lists that they sell.

If Your Identity Is Stolen

If someone has used your personal identification to fraudulently establish credit, report the incident as quickly as possible to each of the three major credit reporting agencies and request that a fraud alert be placed on your file.

Experian	888-397-9742
Equifax	800-525-6285
Trans Union	800-680-7289

Next, obtain a copy of your credit report from each of the credit reporting agencies. Check to see whether any additional accounts were opened without your consent or whether unauthorized charges were billed to your accounts. To request copies of your credit reports, call:

Experian	888-397-3742
Equifax	800-685-1111
Trans Union	800-916-8800

You can also purchase a copy of your credit history and credit score online at www.myfico.com for $12.95. For $49.95, the site will e-mail you whenever there are changes and modifications to your credit report.

Contact the Social Security Administration's Fraud Hotline at 800-269-0271 to report the unauthorized use of your personal identification information. Contact your State Department of Motor Vehicles to see whether the department has issued an unauthorized license number in your name. If so, notify them that you are a victim of identity theft.

File a complaint with the Federal Trade Commission by contacting the FTC's Identity Theft Hotline in the following ways:

Telephone:	877-IDTHEFT (877-438-4338)
TTD:	202-326-2502
Mail:	Identity Theft Clearinghouse
	Federal Trade Commission
	600 Pennsylvania Avenue, NW
	Washington, DC 20590-0001
Web site:	www.consumer.gov/idtheft

The Federal Trade Commission publishes a booklet that can explain more. It's called *ID Theft: When Bad Things Happen to Your Good Name.*

Another good Web site is www.privacyrights.org.

According to the Privacy Rights Clearinghouse and the California Public Interest Research group, identity theft victims spend an average of 175 hours and $808 in out-of-pocket expenses clearing their names. Don't let this happen to you.

SIMPLE STEP

50

GO BACK TO WORK

Some people are born lucky. They're in the right place at the right time. The rest of us just work hard for everything we have.

Crises throw us off the path we're used to treading. Our daily routine is disrupted, and that wreaks havoc with our lives. Although your disaster instinct may tell you to hide under the covers, what may actually be the best thing for you and your finances is to get up and go back to work.

Forcing yourself into a routine, even if it's a new routine, can be healthy. And if your finances are hurting, working part-time or full-time will help. Not only will you bring in some money, but you also won't have as much time to spend. You'll meet new people and stay in contact with your old friends. Your circle of interaction will expand. Organizing your day will help you organize your mind and pass the time. Meanwhile, each day your financial situation continues to improve.

A GOOD START

If you haven't worked in a while, you may want to take stock of everything you can do. Can you type? Write? Draw? Are you computer literate? Can you answer telephones? Check out customers? Sell things?

Many local libraries offer free career guidance and assistance in writing résumés. Some even have career coaches that visit for free one-on-one consultations with library users. Almost all libraries have computers that hook up to the Internet, with librarians who specialize in helping you find things online. In the reference section are shelves of books that analyze companies and can give you ideas on what kind of job might be a good fit for your skills.

If your skills need brushing up, inexpensive classes are available at local community colleges to help teach you how to use computers and the Internet. Or you can take technical classes at a local junior college.

Even in the worst of times, employers are still hiring and there are millions of different jobs that could be right for you. But you'll never know until you try.

TEN FINANCIAL MISTAKES
WE MAKE AFTER A DISASTER

1. Procrastinating

During a financial crisis it's important to do certain things as quickly as possible. For example, it's important to deposit your paychecks, pay your bills, and make the important calls to insurance companies to get the ball rolling. Our instinct is to take cover and protect ourselves, but that can wreak havoc with our financial health. Instead, try to gather all of your energy and force yourself to take care of the financial basics. If you don't, you'll end up dealing with the long-term repercussions of your inaction.

2. Being Disorganized

There's a lot of information in this book on how to get yourself organized. But many people find that once they get themselves organized, they're simply not able to maintain what they've created. So the file structure is there, but there's a stack of papers on the desk just waiting for you to have a free hour, day, week, or month to handle it. Who ever has that kind of time? Although my father always joked that a clean desk was the sign of a sick mind, it's better to be organized. Once a crisis erupts, you'll want to know where all of your documents are as quickly as possible. Develop a plan to maintain your files and contact lists and stick with it. Maybe you'll update these lists twice a year or at major life-changing events. You decide—and then get with the program.

3. Moving Too Quickly

When you've lost it all, you may want to just walk away. Many people do this after a crisis erupts, only to be sorry a year later that they've sold their home or business and moved across the country. You can't run away from your problems, you can only solve them. If you must sell your home to make ends meet, then sell it. But if you can afford to keep it for a year after your financial crisis, try to do that. You may change your mind about "chucking it all" in that time and will have left your options open.

4. Trusting the Wrong People

Scam operators and con artists mill around looking for victims. In the aftermath of a crisis, you're most vulnerable to their sugarcoated promises. When your judgment is impaired, it can also lead you to trust people who, though they offer a legitimate service, may not be particularly good at it: the broker with the brand-name financial firm who really doesn't know what he's doing and blows your inheritance by investing it all in dot-com stocks—or the investment flavor of the day; the insurance salesperson who convinces you that what you really need now is a whole life policy—even if you have no heirs. Before you hand your hard-earned cash over to anybody, check them out. You won't make a mistake by being cautious and doing your homework.

5. Not Paying Your Bills

Credit card, utility, and car companies don't really care how bad a day you're having. They do care that the bills they send are paid promptly. Don't get so overwhelmed by your personal crisis that you forget to pay your bills and balance your checkbook. If you do that, you'll just destroy your credit history, which will make it much more difficult to make a major purchase or refinance your home loan down the line.

6. Failing to Change Names on Accounts

Unless you want mail coming to your deceased or divorced spouse for the rest of your life, you'll need to change the names on your bank, credit card, auto loan, and other financial accounts. In the case of a death or divorce, you're entitled to the same level of credit you had when you were married. The credit card company may try to cancel your account and "give" you your own account. Even if they suggest this, you don't have to go along with it. If the company gives you trouble, call the Federal Trade Commission (toll-free 877-FTC-HELP) and report it.

7. Investing Poorly

A dramatic change in your life will likely change your tolerance for risk when it comes to investing your assets. That's understandable and may even be wise. But you have to understand why you're making certain investment decisions. If you're a new widow and you're at home with young children, you'll want to invest your dollars more conservatively in order to bring in some income but still achieve some growth. On the other hand, if you're terminally ill, the last thing you want to do is lock away your cash in a long-term illiquid investment, like a conservative mutual fund with a 6 percent front or back load (commission). Spending some time with a competent financial planner who can analyze what you have and develop a strategy for getting the most out of your money is one of the smartest things you can do.

8. Overspending

If you're having trouble putting food on the table, you have no business shopping for big-ticket items or buying endless gifts for family and friends. But overspending is one way people react to a dramatic change in their financial lives. If you have the urge to spend and you know you should be conserving capital, consider getting at least a part-time job that will do as much to keep you out of the stores as it will to fatten your wallet.

9. Underinsuring Your Assets

Often after a financial crisis we forget to update our remaining insurance policies. If your spouse had life insurance and it paid off after he or she died, you may now be the sole provider for your children. If that's the case, you may need life insurance to cover the expenses of someone else doing what you're doing to raise them. If your house was destroyed in a fire or tornado, you may need a new home-owner's policy after the home is rebuilt. Take a look at your different policies and try to figure out what kind of insurance is missing. Then plug the gap.

10. Saving the House at the Expense of Everything Else

A very wise real estate agent (okay, it's my mother, Susanne—one of the best real estate agents in Chicago) once told me that a house is a house, but a home is where your heart is. I've taken that to mean that a house is nothing more than four walls, a ceiling, a floor, and some paint. It becomes a home when you and your loved ones move in. (And the same is true for a condo, co-op, or townhouse.) So anyplace you and your loved ones live is your home. Don't become so attached to your house that selling it becomes unthinkable—even if selling it would solve a serious financial crisis. While you should try to wait a year before selling it, there may come a point when selling it will clearly be the answer. You have to ask yourself then if you're better off with the house or without it. I'm guessing that as long as you take your family with you, almost any house will become your home and the center of your family life.

HELPFUL FINANCIAL WEB SITES

These Web sites are among the best out there and can provide excellent advice, calculators, and information about managing and improving your finances. Because Web sites come and go, I've decided to restrict this list to top companies and government departments that have been on the Web for a while. Still, some companies may have gone out of business since the publication of this book.

Commercial Web Sites

Nolo.com	Legal publishing company
Money.com	*Money* magazine and CNN's news department
BankRate.com	Interest rates and information
Homeowners.com	Interest rates and calculators
Morningstar.com	Mutual fund research
Worth.com	*Worth* magazine
SmartMoney.com	*SmartMoney* magazine
MyFico.com	Get your own credit history and credit score
MSN.com	Microsoft's Money Central

AARP.org	American Association of Retired Persons
Reverse.org	Best reverse mortgage Web site
Insure.com	Insurance News Network
III.org	Insurance Information Institute
Quotesmith.com	Buy cheap insurance policies online
Quicken.com	Financial information, loans, insurance

Government Web Sites

FTC.gov	Federal Trade Commission
HUD.gov	Department of Housing and Urban Development
IRS.gov	Internal Revenue Service
Ustreas.gov	Treasury Department—buy bonds direct online
FEMA.gov	Federal Emergency Management Administration

Of course, there are millions of Web sites on the Internet, and you should tap into them if you don't find what you need here or elsewhere in the book. Try my favorite search machine, Google.com.

Glossary of Terms

Abstract (of Title)   A summary of the public records affecting the title to a particular piece of land. An attorney or title insurance company officer creates the abstract of title by examining all recorded instruments (documents) relating to a specific piece of property, such as easements, liens, mortgages, etc.

Accelerated Benefit   A rider that allows a terminally ill person to cash in a policy before he or she dies and collect up to 95 percent of the policy's face value (the stated amount of the policy).

Acceleration Clause   A provision in a loan agreement that allows the lender to require the balance of the loan to become due immediately if mortgage payments are not made or there is a breach in your obligation under your mortgage or note.

Accumulation Fund   The savings component of a universal life insurance policy. The money in this fund earns interest and goes to pay the higher cost of the mortality charge as you age. As long as you pay enough to fund the mortality charge, you can skip payments if your funds dry up. And, if you contribute enough to the accumulation fund early on and you get a few good years of interest, that interest may be enough to pay the premium later on.

Acquisition or Bank Fee   The average fee you'll pay to a car dealer at the start of a car lease. Typically it is $300 to $400, and is not negotiable.

Addendum   Any addition to, or modification of, a contract. Also called an *amendment* or *rider*.

Adjustable-Rate Mortgage (ARM)   A type of loan whose prevailing interest rate is tied to an economic index (like one-year Treasury Bills), which fluctuates with the market. The three most popular types of ARMs are one-year ARMs, which adjust every year, three-year ARMs, which adjust every three years, and five-year ARMs, which adjust every five years. When the loan adjusts, the lender tacks a margin onto the economic index rate to come up with your loan's new rate. ARMs are considered riskier than fixed-rate mortgages, but their starting interest rates are generally lower than a longer-term rate, and in the past five to ten years, people have done very well with them.

Adjusted Gross Income   Your total income reduced by contributions to retirement accounts, alimony payments, and certain other exclusions.

Agency   A term used to describe the relationship between a home seller and a real estate broker, or a homebuyer and a real estate broker.

Agency Closing   The lender's use of a title company or other party to act on the lender's behalf for the purposes of closing on the purchase of a home or refinancing of a home loan.

Agent   An individual who acts on behalf of a consumer. A real estate agent represents a buyer or a seller in the purchase or sale of a home. Licensed by the state, a real estate agent must work for a broker or a brokerage firm. An insurance agent helps a consumer purchase an insurance policy. Insurance agents are also licensed by the state.

Agreement of Sale   This document is also known as the contract of purchase, purchase agreement, or sales agreement. It is the agreement by which the seller agrees to sell you his or her property if you pay a certain price. It contains all the provisions and conditions for the purchase, must be written, and is signed by both parties.

Amortization   A payment plan that enables the borrower to repay his debt gradually through monthly payments of principal and interest. Amortization tables allow you to see exactly how much you would pay each month in interest and how much you repay in principal, depending on the amount of money borrowed at a specific interest rate.

Annual Mileage Allowance   The number of miles included as part of a car lease. Car dealers will offer as few miles as they can get away with, perhaps as few as 10,000 per year, or 30,000 over a three-year lease. But they will go as high as 15,000 miles per year if you negotiate it. You'll pay anywhere from 10 cents to 50 cents for each additional mile you drive over the limit, so negotiate mileage (and think carefully about how far you drive before you negotiate).

Annual Percentage Rate (APR)   The total cost of a loan, expressed as a percentage rate of interest, which includes not only the loan's interest rate, but factors in all the costs associated with making that loan, including closing costs and fees. The costs are then amortized over the life of the loan. Banks are required by the federal Truth-in-Lending statutes to disclose the APR of a loan, which allows borrowers to better compare various loans from different lenders.

Any-Occupation Policy   A type of private disability insurance that pays if—from the insurer's perspective—you can't work at any job for which your education and training qualify you.

Application A series of documents you must fill out when you apply for a home loan or insurance policies.

Application Fee A onetime fee charged by a company for processing your application for a loan. For a home loan, the application fee is sometimes applied toward certain costs, including the appraisal and credit report.

Appraisal The opinion of an appraiser, who estimates the value of a home at a specific point in time for the purpose of financing or refinancing a home.

Articles-of-Agreement for Deed A type of seller financing that allows the buyer to purchase the home in installments over a specified period of time. The seller keeps legal title to the home until the loan is paid off. The buyer receives an interest in the property—called equitable title—but does not own it. However, because the buyer is paying the real estate taxes and paying interest to the seller, it is the buyer who receives the tax benefits of home ownership.

Asset Allocation A term used to express your choice among different types of asset classes and styles. You might have growth or value funds, which are mutual funds typically focused on companies that are growing quickly or companies that are perhaps out of favor temporarily and are typically priced cheaply relative to their assets, profits, and potential. Value funds are betting that these stocks have a lot of room to grow. Your fund may be international (holding shares of international companies) or domestic (holding shares of U.S. companies only). It might be large-cap (focused on huge corporations), mid-cap (medium-sized companies), or small-cap (smaller companies).

Assumption of Mortgage   If you assume a mortgage when you purchase a home, you undertake to fulfill the obligations of the existing loan agreement the seller made with the lender. The obligations are similar to those that you would incur if you took out a new mortgage. When assuming a mortgage, you become personally liable for the payment of principal and interest. The seller, or original mortgagor, is released from the liability, and should get that release in writing. Otherwise, he or she could be liable if you don't make the monthly payments.

Balloon Mortgage   A type of mortgage that is generally short in length, but is amortized over twenty-five or thirty years so the borrower pays a combination of interest and principal each month. At the end of the loan term, the entire balance of the loan must be repaid at once.

Blue Chips   Large, well-established companies that offer investors some growth with a solid dividend. Companies listed on the S&P 500 are frequently referred to as blue chip stocks, capable of weathering even the worst market fluctuations.

Bond   A government's (federal or municipal) or a corporation's obligation to repay you your principal plus a certain amount of interest over a fixed period of time.

Bond Fund   A bond fund is a shorthand way of talking about a mutual fund made up of bond issues.

Broker, Real Estate   An individual who acts as the agent of the seller or buyer. A real estate broker must be licensed by the state.

Broker, Stocks   An individual who helps consumers purchase equities, like stocks and bonds. A stockbroker must be licensed.

Building Line or **Setback**   The distance from the front, back, or side of a lot, beyond which construction or improvements may not extend without permission by the proper governmental authority or other party. The building line may be established by a filed plat of subdivision, by restrictive covenants in deeds, by building codes, or by zoning ordinances.

Buy Down   An incentive offered by a developer or home seller that allows the homebuyer to lower his or her initial interest rate by putting up a certain amount of money. A buy down also refers to the process of paying extra points up front at the closing of your loan in order to have a lower interest rate over the life of the loan.

Buyer Broker   A buyer broker is a real estate broker who specializes in representing buyers. Unlike a seller broker or conventional broker, the buyer broker has a fiduciary duty to the buyer, because the buyer accepts the legal obligation of paying the broker. The buyer broker is obligated to find the best property for a client, and then negotiate the best possible purchase price and terms. Buyer brokerage has gained a significant amount of respect in recent years, since the National Association of Realtors has changed its code of ethics to accept this designation.

Buyer's Market   Conditions that favor the buyer. A buyer's market usually occurs when there are too many homes for sale, and a home can be bought for less money.

Callability   A bond may be called in before it is due. This means the issuer of the bond may decide to refinance its debt and pay back all of the bond holders early. If interest rates fall, the chances of a bond being called increase because the bond holder could simply refinance the debt for less money (like you'd refinance your mortgage if rates dropped).

Calls   When a company orders preferred stock or bond holders turn in their stock or bonds for money.

Capital Gain   A profit made on the sale of stocks, bonds, real estate, or other assets.

Capitalized Cost or **Gross Capitalized Cost**   This is the price of the car that the dealer uses to construct the lease. It also includes all the items and services that come with the car in the lease. A crucial number, it is negotiable.

Capitalized Cost Reduction   Your down payment for the purchase of a car. It is negotiable. If you're trading in a car, the value of the trade-in should be applied to either the capitalized cost reduction or your monthly payments.

Capital Loss   The loss taken on the sale of stocks, bonds, real estate, or other assets.

Certificate of Title   A document or instrument issued by a local government agency to an owner, naming the owner as the owner of an automobile or boat. When the item is sold, the certificate of title is transferred to the buyer. The agency then issues a new certificate of title to the buyer.

Cash Surrender Value (Cash Value)   The amount available in cash upon voluntary termination of an insurance policy by its owner before it becomes payable by death or maturity. This amount is typically paid in cash or paid-up insurance.

Cash Value Policy   A category of life insurance, including whole life, universal life, and variable universal life, that combines the death benefit with a savings component. The insurance policy is broken down into two parts: the mortality charge (the part that pays for the death benefit) and a reserve (the savings component that earns interest). As you get older, the cost of the death benefit rises. In addition to interest, the reserve might receive an annual dividend, depending on how many policies have been paid out and how well the insurer has invested the premiums it has received.

Catastrophic Care Most health insurance policies cover catastrophic care, including such procedures as transplants, complex neonatal care, severe burns care, or trauma care.

Chain of Title The lineage of ownership of a particular property.

Churning Also known as twisting, churning is an attempt by an unscrupulous agent from an insurance company to cancel your existing policy and replace it with a new one, drawing down your cash value (called "juice" in industry jargon) to pay for it. This activity generates additional commission for the agent and may result in your having to pay more down the line. It is also a word used to describe the actions of a stockbroker who continually buys and sells for an account; churning profits for the broker often eats up whatever profits might be there for the consumer.

Classified Shares Mutual fund shares grouped alphabetically. "A" shares are traditional "load" funds, where you pay the broker right off the top of your investment. "B" shares still pay a commission, but the mutual fund puts up the money and then gradually withdraws it from your account. "C" and "D" shares are sometimes called level-load funds. The broker gets no commission up front, but instead gets an annual fee (called a trail commission) from the investor's account.

Closed-Ended A mutual fund that has closed its doors to new investors and their cash in order to maintain its size and position in the market.

Code-and-Condition Coverage (Building Code Coverage) A homeowner's insurance rider that covers the cost of meeting new building codes that may have gone into effect after your home was built, and to which any new homes built are subject. Also known as an *ordinance-and-law rider*.

Common Stock   A share of ownership in a company.

Conditionally Renewable Policy   A type of private disability insurance policy that may be renewed at the insurer's discretion.

Consumer Federation of America (CFA)   A nonprofit association of consumer interest groups that works to further the consumer interest through educational programs and advocacy. The CFA pays particular attention to those in need, including children, elderly persons living on fixed incomes, and the poor.

Consumer Price Index (CPI)   A measure of the changes in price of all the goods and services that urban households purchase for consumption. The CPI is used as an economic indicator, a policy guide, a means to adjust income payments for inflation, and a means to determine the cost of school lunches, among other uses.

Contrarian Fund   A contrarian fund is a stock mutual fund that is positioned against conventional wisdom. When Asia was headed into a recession during the late 1990s, for example, contrarian international funds went in and began swooping up the stocks of companies, betting that they'd come back.

Cost-of-Living Adjustment (COLA)   A rider that can be added to a long-term care policy under which the policy owner's benefits increase to keep pace with the consumer price index (CPI).

Convertible Bond   A bond that can be converted into shares of stock in a corporation.

Corporate Bond   A bond issued by a corporation.

Coupon   The actual interest payment made on each bond. If you have a $5,000 bond paying 7 percent interest, you will receive $350 each year, most likely in two $175 payments. The $350 is the coupon. The interest rate of the bond is also referred to as the *coupon rate*. The name originates from how you used to collect your interest (and still do on some). You'd actually clip a coupon and bring it in to receive your interest. Today, this is often done electronically, with the interest simply deposited in your bank account.

Current Yield   The coupon interest payment divided by the bond's price. This will fluctuate based on where interest rates are and what you could currently sell your bond for in the marketplace.

Debt Service   The total amount of debt (credit cards, mortgage, car loan) that an individual is carrying at any one time.

Deferred Compensation Plan   Employees may put a limited portion of their pretax earnings into a deferred compensation plan, like a 401(k) or Keogh. The earnings are excluded from tax calculations and grow tax-free until the funds are withdrawn at retirement.

Dependent   An individual for whom the taxpayer provides over half of the support for the calendar year. This could be a child, spouse, relative, or nonrelative living as a member of the taxpayer's household.

Discount   Newly issued bonds are typically sold at some sort of discount. A bond that has a face value of $1,000 and sells for $925, for example, has a $75 discount. When interest rates rise, bonds are discounted more because you need a less expensive bond to achieve the same interest rate.

Diversified Funds   According to the Diversified Mutual Fund Investment Act of 1940, a mutual fund calling itself diversified must spread its assets around. Seventy-five percent of its assets must be divvied up so no more than 5 percent of the fund's assets are invested in a single stock. Funds that do not call themselves diversified may invest a larger percent of their holdings in a single stock.

Dividends   A shareholder's share of a company's profits, typically paid out in quarterly installments. To find out how much you'll receive, multiply the dividend (published in your local paper) by the number of shares you own.

Endorsement   An amendment to an insurance policy, usually by means of a rider.

Equity   Your share of ownership in a company. Stockholders are often referred to as *equity investors*, because they invest in the equity of a company.

Estimated Tax Payments   If you are self-employed, or have significant dividend income or investment income in addition to your regular salary, you must make tax payments based on the estimated tax you'll owe at the end of the year. Your estimated tax payments must equal either 100 percent of the tax you paid in the previous year or 90 percent of your total tax for the current year.

Exemption (Tax)   You may take a tax exemption from your adjusted gross income for yourself, your spouse, and any dependents. The tax exemption basically excludes money from taxation.

Fee Simple   The most basic type of ownership, under which the owner has the right to use and dispose of the property at will.

Fiduciary Duty   A relationship of trust between a broker and a seller, or a buyer broker and a buyer, or an attorney and a client.

Filing Status A declaration as to your personal status (i.e., married, single, separated, dependents or not). Your filing status will determine your standard deduction, the tax rate table you'll use to compute your tax liability, and the deductions and credits to which you're entitled.

First Mortgage A mortgage that takes priority over all other voluntary liens.

Fixture Personal property, such as a built-in bookcase, furnace, hot water heater, and recessed lights, that becomes "affixed" because it has been permanently attached to the home.

Foreclosure The legal action taken to extinguish a homeowner's right and interest in a property, so that the property can be sold in a foreclosure sale to satisfy a debt.

401(k) Plan A defined contribution plan for employees. Some companies do not offer this benefit, but if they do, you may contribute up to a maximum set by the government and indexed to inflation. As an additional benefit, some employers match contributions up to a certain dollar limit or percentage.

403(b) Plan A retirement plan offered by certain religious, charitable, or public organizations. It operates much like a 401(k) plan.

Fund of Funds A mutual fund that is made up of other mutual funds. The idea here is that you are not diversified enough by choosing a diversified mutual fund, so you buy one fund that diversifies by purchasing several different funds.

Fund Supermarket A relatively new concept, a fund supermarket is an investment firm (often called a *family*) that offers not only its own mutual funds, but the ability to invest in the mutual funds of other families. A benefit to this is that all of your investments in these funds would be displayed on one statement from your primary family. On the down side, sometimes supermarkets will tack on additional charges for investing in funds outside the family if that fund doesn't separately pay a commission.

GAP Insurance   This stands for *guaranteed auto protection*, and you need it if you're leasing. This insurance will pay the balance on the lease and the early termination penalties if the car is stolen or totaled. Negotiate to have it included with your lease payment.

Gift Letter   A letter to the lender indicating that a gift of cash has been made to the buyer and that it is not expected to be repaid. The letter must detail the amount of the gift and the name of the giver.

Good Faith Estimate (GFE)   Under the Real Estate Settlement Procedures Act (RESPA), lenders are required to give potential borrowers a written good faith estimate of closing costs within three days of an application submission.

Grace Period   The period of time after a loan payment due date in which a mortgage payment may be made and not be considered delinquent.

Graduated Payment Mortgage   A mortgage in which the payments increase over the life of the mortgage, allowing the borrower to make very low payments at the beginning of the loan.

Growth Stock   A company that is focusing on growing above all else. All profits are typically reinvested into the company to keep it growing quickly, so little if any dividends are paid.

Guaranteed Cost Replacement   A type of homeowner's insurance that guarantees to rebuild your home no matter what the cost and has a rider built in to take care of inflation. On some policies, insurers might only pay to rebuild your home up to 120 to 125 percent of your policy amount. It's up to you to stay on top of how much it will cost to rebuild your home.

Guaranteed Renewable Policy   An insurance policy that must be renewed as long as the insured pays the premium on time. Typically, an insurer cannot make any changes to a guaranteed renewable policy other than to increase the premium rate for an entire class of policy holders.

Hard Asset Funds   A mutual fund that holds a portion of its assets in gold or silver, or similar commodities, or in indices that are based on hard assets. Hard asset funds may also be invested in real estate.

Hazard Insurance   Insurance that covers the property from damages that might materially affect its value. Also see *homeowner's insurance*.

Health Insurance Portability and Accountability Act Effective July 1, 1997, this act specifies that if a person has been covered by insurance during the past twelve months, a new insurer cannot refuse to cover that person nor can it force him or her to accept a waiting period when joining a new group plan.

HMO (Health Maintenance Organization)   An organization that provides a wide range of comprehensive health care services for a specified group at a fixed periodic payment. An HMO can be sponsored by the government, medical schools, hospitals, employers, labor unions, consumer groups, insurance companies, and hospital-medical plans.

Holdback An amount of money held back at closing by the lender or the escrow agent until a particular condition has been met. If the problem is a repair, the money is kept until the repair is made. If the repair is not made, the lender or escrow agent uses the money to make the repair. Buyers and sellers may also have holdbacks between them, to ensure that specific conditions of the sale are met.

Homeowners' Association A group of homeowners in a particular subdivision or area who band together to take care of common property and common interests.

Homeowner's Insurance Coverage that includes hazard insurance as well as personal liability and theft.

Home Warranty A service contract that covers appliances (with exclusions) in working condition in the home for a certain period of time, usually one year. Homeowners are responsible for a per-call service fee. There is a homeowner's warranty for new construction. Some developers will purchase a warranty from a company specializing in new construction for the homes they sell. A homeowner's warranty will warrant the good working order of the appliances and workmanship of a new home for between one and ten years; for example, appliances might be covered for one year, while the roof may be covered for several years.

Hostile Takeover When a company purchases another against the will of the purchased company's management.

Housing and Urban Development, Department of Also known as HUD, this is the federal department responsible for the nation's housing programs. It also regulates RESPA, the Real Estate Settlement Procedures Act, which governs how lenders must deal with their customers.

Inception Fees These are the fees the car dealer will require you to pay, including your first monthly payment, refundable security deposit, Department of Motor Vehicle (DMV) fees, and possibly an acquisition fee. You'll have to come up with this cash up front, even if you're getting a "no money down" lease. If you're paying a down payment, you'll have to add that in as well.

Income Replacement Policy A category of private disability insurance that covers the difference between what you earned prior to the disability and what you now earn doing a different job.

Income Stock A company that tends to pay out more of its profits to shareholders (in the form of dividends) and put less toward growth.

Indemnity Plans A type of health care insurance set up as a fee-for-service plan. You get something done, you pay for it. Typically there are no restrictions on care, and the plan coverage kicks in when you reach a certain deductible. Unlike an HMO, you (or the doctor's office) will also have to bill the insurance company. An advantage to indemnity plans is that you can see the doctor you choose and seek second opinions or specialists anywhere in the country. On the other hand, it's the most expensive way to go, and not every employer offers this plan.

Index Funds These are stock mutual funds designed to mimic the movements of a particular index. For example, a fund trying to mimic the movement of the Standard & Poor's (S&P) 500 will either purchase every stock on the S&P 500 in the same ratio that those stocks appear on the index, or will purchase a representative sample of companies that closely approximate the index. Since index funds rarely change their holdings, they are typically cheap to hold and may do better for investors over the long haul.

Individual Retirement Account (IRA)   An account to which any individual who earns income may contribute up to $2,000 per year. The contributions are tax-deductible, and the earnings grow tax-free, although they may be taxed upon withdrawal.

Initial Public Offering (IPO)   A young company hoping to finance future growth will often go public to raise additional funds. Many IPOs rise dramatically the first day of the offering, then settle back down to a more reasonable share price. Some investors try to get in on the ground floor of an IPO and then sell their shares within the first day or week.

Inspection, Home   The service a professional home inspector performs when he or she is hired to scrutinize the home for any possible structural defects. May also be done in order to check for the presence of toxic substances, such as leaded paint or water, asbestos, radon, or pests, including termites.

Installment Contract for Deed   The purchase of property in installments. Title to the property is given to the purchaser when all installments are made.

Institutional Investors or Lenders   Private or public companies, corporations, or funds (such as pension funds) that purchase loans on the secondary market from commercial lenders such as banks and savings and loans. Or, they are sources of funds for mortgages through mortgage brokers.

Interest   Money charged for the use of borrowed funds. Usually expressed as an interest rate, it is the percentage of the total loan charged annually for the use of the funds.

Interest-Only Mortgage   A loan in which only the interest is paid on a regular basis (usually monthly), and the principal is owed in full at the end of the loan term.

Interest Rate Cap The total number of percentage points that an adjustable-rate mortgage (ARM) might rise over the life of the loan.

Joint Tenancy An equal, undivided ownership in a property taken by two or more owners. Under joint tenancy there are rights of survivorship, which means that if one of the owners dies, the surviving owner, rather than the heirs of the estate, inherits the other's total interest in the property.

Keogh A retirement plan for employees of unincorporated businesses or for self-employed individuals. You may contribute up to 25 percent of your earned income, to a maximum of $30,000.

Landscape The trees, flowers, planting, lawn, and shrubbery that surround the exterior of a dwelling.

Late Charge A penalty applied to a mortgage payment that arrives after the grace period (usually the tenth or fifteenth of a month).

Lease Charge or **Money Factor** This is the complicated way car dealers calculate lease payments. Similar to an interest rate, you should multiply the money factor by 2,400 to approximate the annual percentage rate of your lease. It is not negotiable, but differs from lease to lease, car to car, and company to company. Usually it is not disclosed, since car companies are not required to do so under *Regulation M.*

Lease with an Option to Buy When the renter or lessee of a piece of property has the right to purchase the property for a specific period of time at a specific price. Usually, a lease with an option to buy allows a first-time buyer to accumulate a down payment by applying a portion of the monthly rent toward the down payment.

Lender A person, company, corporation, or entity that lends money for the purchase of real estate.

Lessee The person leasing a vehicle or residence.

Lessor The landlord or leasing company, bank or finance company, that leases the car or apartment to you.

Letter of Intent A formal statement, usually in letter form, from the buyer to the seller stating that the buyer intends to purchase a specific piece of property for a specific price on a specific date.

Leverage Using a small amount of cash, say a 10 or 20 percent down payment, to purchase a piece of property.

Lien An encumbrance against the property, which may be voluntary or involuntary. There are many different kinds of liens, including a tax lien (for unpaid federal, state, or real estate taxes), a judgment lien (for monetary judgments by a court of law), a mortgage lien (when you take out a mortgage), and a mechanic's lien (for work done by a contractor on the property that has not been paid for). For a lien to be attached to the property's title, it must usually be filed or recorded with a local county government office.

Life Cycle Funds These are mutual funds specifically designed to mirror what many experts feel are optimum ratios of stocks and bonds throughout the different stages in your life. You may be able to choose from three or four funds, one designed for twenty- to thirty-year-olds, one for forty- to fifty-year-olds, and so on.

Listing A property that a broker agrees to list for sale in return for a commission.

Load A sales charge on a mutual fund that can range from 1 to 7 percent. It might be a front load (payable when you buy into the fund) or a back load (payable when you cash out). You typically pay this because you want the service of a financial professional selecting and building your portfolio. Your load may decrease the longer you hold the fund. If you cashed out in the first year, you'd pay 6 percent. Cash out three years later and the load may only be 3 percent.

Loan An amount of money that is loaned to a borrower, who agrees to repay it plus interest.

Loan Commitment A written document that states that a mortgage company has agreed to lend a buyer a certain amount of money at a certain rate of interest for a specific period of time. It may contain sets of conditions and a date by which the loan must close.

Loan Origination Fee A onetime fee charged by the mortgage company to arrange the financing for the loan.

Loan-to-Value Ratio The ratio of the amount of money you wish to borrow compared to the value of the property you wish to purchase. Institutional investors (who buy loans on the secondary market from your mortgage company) set up certain ratios that guide lending practices. For example, the mortgage company might lend you only 80 percent of a property's value.

Location Where property is geographically situated. "Location, location, location" is a broker's maxim that states that where the property is located is its most important feature, because you can change everything about a house except its location.

Lock-In The mechanism by which a borrower locks in the interest rate that will be charged on a particular loan. Usually, the lock lasts for a certain time period, such as thirty, forty-five, or sixty days. On a new construction, the lock may be much longer.

Long-Term Care Insurance Insurance that covers the cost of long-term care in a nursing home, other custodial care settings, or at home.

Maintenance Fee The monthly or annual fee charged to condo, co-op, or town-house owners and paid to the home-owner's association, for the maintenance of common property. Also called an *assessment*.

Management Buyout When the individuals running a company get together, borrow money, and buy most or all of its common shares.

Market Price On any given day, your bond will be worth more or less than the face value. That's because the bond market is continually active, with traders bidding up and down the value of bonds based on the current interest rate of the day. When interest rates rise, bonds are worth less (because it takes a smaller amount of capital to earn the same amount of interest). When interest rates fall, bonds are worth more (because it takes a greater amount of money to earn the same amount of interest).

Market Sector The categorizing of companies based on the industry in which they operate. Some sectors include technology and transportation.

Matured Bond A bond that has been paid back in full, or is due for full payment.

Medicaid State public assistance programs to persons who are unable to pay for health care. Title XIX of the federal Social Security Act provides matching federal funds for financing state Medicaid programs.

Medicare A program of Hospital Insurance (Part A) and Supplementary Medical Insurance (Part B) protection provided under the Social Security Act.

Medicare Supplemental Insurance (Medigap or Med-Sup)   A term used in reference to private insurance products that supplement Medicare insurance benefits.

Merger   When two companies voluntarily join together. Sometimes mergers are really takeovers, where one company ends up becoming the dominant presence.

Mortgage   A document granting a lien on a home in exchange for financing granted by a lender. The mortgage is the means by which the lender secures the loan and has the ability to foreclose on the home.

Mortgage Banker   A company or a corporation, like a bank, that lends its own funds to borrowers in addition to bringing together lenders and borrowers. A mortgage banker may also service the loan (i.e., collect the monthly payments).

Mortgage Broker   A company or individual that brings together lenders and borrowers and processes mortgage applications.

Mortgagee   A legal term for the lender.

Mortgagor   A legal term for the borrower.

Multiple Listing Service (MLS)   A computerized listing of all properties offered for sale by member brokers. Buyers may gain access to the MLS only by working with a member broker.

Municipal Bond   A bond offered by a local municipality. Munis, as they are commonly known, are not taxed by the federal government.

Negative Amortization   A condition created when the monthly mortgage payment is less than the amount necessary to pay off the loan over the period of time set forth in the note. Because you're paying less than the amount necessary, the actual loan amount increases over time. That's how you end up with negative equity. To pay off the loan, a lump-sum payment may have to be made.

Net Asset Value (NAV) The value per share of a mutual fund. This is similar to a stock price.

No-Fault Insurance A legal policy adopted by some states that abolishes liability for a death or injury caused by a motor vehicle regardless of the accident's cause. An injured party cannot sue another driver unless a particular crime or hazard is proven. Drivers in states with no-fault insurance laws can buy *personal injury protection*, which means you pay for your injuries and the other driver pays for his or her injuries.

No-Load These are mutual funds that charge no fees to buy in or cash out. There are other charges, however. Check the funds *expense ratio* to find out how much you're being charged.

Non-Cancellable Policy A policy specifying that, as long as you pay your premiums on time, the insurer can't raise your premium and can't cancel your policy.

Open-Ended This is a mutual fund that continues to welcome new investors and their cash.

Open-End Lease When you bring the car back, the dealer compares the actual value of the car with the residual value stated in your lease contract. If the actual value is less than the stated residual value, you make up the difference. If, by chance, the car has retained more of its value, the dealer pays you.

Operating Expense Ratio (OER) Also known as the expense ratio, the OER is the cost of administering and managing a mutual fund, including salaries and bonuses paid. This can run .05 to 3 percent per year.

Option to Purchase Also known as a *lease/option*, this is when a buyer pays for the right or option to purchase property for a given length of time, without having the obligation to actually purchase the property.

Optionally Renewable Policy A contract of health insurance in which the insurer reserves the right to terminate the coverage at any anniversary or, in some cases, at any premium due date, but does not have the right to terminate coverage between such dates.

Ordinance-and-Law Rider See *Code-and-Condition Coverage*

Origination Fee A fee charged by the lender for allowing you to borrow money to purchase property. The fee—which is also referred to as *points*—is usually expressed as a percentage of the total loan amount.

Ownership The absolute right to use, enjoy, and dispose of property. You own it!

Own-Occupation Policy A type of private disability insurance that pays if you can't work at your specific job.

Package Mortgage A mortgage that uses both real and personal property to secure a loan.

Paper Slang usage that refers to the mortgage, trust deed, installment, and land contract.

Par A bond's face value. A $1,000 bond, for example, will have a par value of $1,000. The term *par* may be a bit confusing because even if your bond is worth $10,000, par also refers to 100, as in 100 percent of a bond's value. So you may hear that your bond cost 95, which means 95 percent of par.

That means you'll get a 5 percent discount, and pay $950 for every bond with a $1,000 face value. If the bond cost 116, that means it's 116 percent of par, or cost you $1,160 for a bond with a face value of $1,000

Partial Disability Coverage   A benefit sometimes found in disability income policies providing for the payment of reduced monthly income in the event the insured cannot work full time and/or is prevented from performing one or more important daily duties pertaining to his or her occupation.

Penalty (IRS)   A fine levied by the IRS. You may pay a flat dollar fee or a fee based on an interest charge for unpaid taxes, failure to pay taxes, failure to make estimated tax payments, failure to make federal tax deposits, or filing late.

Personal Articles Rider   Coverage designed to insure property of a movable nature. The coverage typically protects against all physical loss, subject to special exclusions and conditions.

Personal Injury Protection   First-party no-fault coverage in which an insurer pays, within the specified limits, the wage loss, medical, hospital, and funeral expenses of the insured.

Personal Property   Movable property, such as appliances, furniture, clothing, and artwork.

PITI   An acronym for "principal, interest, taxes, and insurance." These are usually the four parts of your monthly mortgage payment.

Pledged Account   Borrowers who do not want to have a real estate tax or insurance escrow administered by the mortgage servicer can, in some circumstances, pledge a savings account into which enough money to cover real estate taxes and the insurance premium must be deposited. You must then make the payments for your real estate taxes and insurance premiums from a separate account. If you fail to pay your taxes or premiums, the lender is allowed to use the funds in the pledged account to make those payments.

Point   A point is 1 percent of the loan amount.

POS (Point of Service) Plans   A health insurance plan that permits an individual to choose providers outside the plan yet encourages the use of network providers. This type of plan is also known as an open-ended HMO or PPO.

Possession   Being in control of a piece of property, and having the right to use it to the exclusion of all others.

Power of Attorney   The legal authorization given to an individual to act on behalf of another individual.

PPO (Preferred Provider Organization)   An arrangement whereby a third-party payer contracts with a group of medical care providers who furnish services at lower than usual fees in return for prompt payment and a certain volume of patients.

Pre-Existing Condition   A physical condition that existed before the effective date of coverage.

Preferred Stock   A special class of stock that may have certain voting privileges. Companies typically pay a fixed, high dividend whose return is similar to what you'd get on a bond. While the price of preferred stock can rise, common stock prices typically rise faster than preferred stock.

Prepaid Interest   Interest paid at closing for the number of days left in the month after closing. For example, if you close on the fifteenth, you would prepay the interest for the fifteenth through the end of the month.

Prepayment Penalty   A fine imposed when a loan is paid off before it comes due. Many states now have laws against prepayment penalties, although banks with federal charters claim to be exempt from state laws. If possible, do not use a mortgage that has a prepayment penalty, or you will be charged a fine if you sell your property before your mortgage has been paid off.

Prequalifying for a Loan   When a mortgage company tells a buyer in advance of the formal application approximately how much money the buyer can afford to borrow.

Presumptive Disability   A type of private disability insurance that presumes its holder to be fully disabled and entitled to full benefits if he or she loses his or her sight, speech, hearing, or some other specified faculty.

Price to Earnings Ratio (P/E)   This is the price of a stock divided by a company's earnings per share. Typically, newspapers will publish a company's P/E ratio in the stock market tables. When a company's stock has a high P/E ratio, its earnings have risen rapidly and investors have bid up the price of the stock even higher, guessing that continued high growth is in the company's future.

Principal   If you're getting a home loan, the principal is the amount of money you borrow. If you're buying a bond, the principal is the amount you're lending. Typically, you'll buy bonds with a face value of $1,000. If you buy a $1,000 bond, your principal is $1,000.

Private Mortgage Insurance (PMI)   Special insurance that specifically protects the top 20 percent of a loan, allowing the lender to lend more than 80 percent of the value of the property. PMI is paid in monthly installments by the borrower, and is for the benefit of the lender, not the buyer.

Property Tax   A tax levied by a county or local authority on the value of real estate.

Proration   The proportional division of certain costs of home ownership. Usually used at closing to figure out how much the buyer and seller each owe for certain expenditures, including real estate taxes, assessments, and water bills.

Purchase Agreement   An agreement between the buyer and seller for the purchase of property.

Purchase Fee   This is a fee you'll pay in addition to the purchase option price if you do decide to purchase your leased car at the end of the lease term. Typically, it's about $250 to $300 and it is negotiable.

Purchase Money Mortgage   An instrument used in seller financing, a purchase money mortgage is signed by a buyer and given to the seller in exchange for a portion of the purchase price.

Purchase-Option Price   The price you'll pay to buy the car at the end of the lease. Typically, it's not negotiable, but it may be tied into the number of miles you're allotted each year. A car that's driven 15,000 miles a year will be less valuable than a car driven only 10,000 miles a year.

Quit-Claim Deed   A deed that operates to release any interest in a property that a person may have, *without a representation that he or she actually has a right in that property*. For example, Sally may use a quit-claim deed to grant Bill her interest in the White House, in Washington, D.C., although she may not actually own or have any rights to that particular house.

Real Rate of Return   Your rate of return with a bond consists of two pieces: the interest you've earned on the bond, and the actual market value of the bond (it could be above or below face value when you sell it). If the market value of the bond has appreciated, you may have to pay capital gains on the rise in value. The interest you earn is taxed like income.

Real Estate   Land and anything permanently attached to it, such as buildings and improvements.

Real Estate Agent   An individual licensed by the state, who acts on behalf of the seller or buyer. For his or her services, the agent receives a commission, which is usually expressed as a percentage of the sales price of a home and is split with his or her real estate firm. A real estate agent must either be a real estate broker or work for one.

Real Estate Attorney   An attorney who specializes in the purchase and sale of real estate.

Real Estate Broker   An individual who is licensed by the state to act as an agent on behalf of the seller or buyer. For his or her services, the broker receives a commission, which is usually expressed as a percentage of the sales price of a home.

Real Estate Settlement Procedures Act (RESPA)   This federal statute was originally passed in 1974, and contains provisions that govern the way companies involved with a real estate closing must treat each other and the consumer. For example, one section of RESPA requires lenders to give consumers a written good faith estimate within three days of making an application for a loan. Another section of RESPA prohibits title companies from giving referral fees to brokers for steering business to them.

Realtist   A designation given to an agent or broker who is a member of the National Association of Real Estate Brokers.

Realtor A designation given to a real estate agent or broker who is a member of the National Association of Realtors.

Recording The process of filing documents at a specific government office. Upon such recording, the document becomes part of the public record.

Redemption Fee Typically a charge that's imposed on people who redeem their shares within a short period of time. It might be ninety days or three years. Some funds impose a .25 percent redemption fee no matter when you cash out. Why? This is another way for funds to be profitable. But there may be some additional costs if too many people take their money out at exactly the same moment. Funds have to keep some money in cash reserves in case people want to redeem their shares. If too many people want to redeem their shares all at once, the fund would have to sell some stock, perhaps at not the most fortuitous time.

Redlining The slang term used to describe an illegal practice of discrimination against a particular racial group by real estate lenders or insurance companies. Redlining occurs when lenders or insurance companies decide certain areas of a community are too high risk. Real estate companies who redline simply refuse to give a mortgage to buyers who want to purchase property in those areas, regardless of their qualifications or creditworthiness. Insurance companies who redline refuse to insure consumers who live in certain neighborhoods.

Regulation M The revised federal rules that went into effect at the end of 1997. Regulation M standardized and simplified car leasing forms and language. While it requires dealers to disclose all sorts of information, it does not require them to disclose the money factor (also known as the lease rate).

Regulation Z Also known as the Truth in Lending Act. Congress determined that lenders must provide a written good faith estimate of closing costs to all borrowers and provide them with other written information about the loan.

Replacement Insurance Guarantees that the insurer will pay for the cost of replacing the home in its current condition up to the policy's limits. This is a less expensive form of homeowner's insurance than *guaranteed cost replacement insurance* (which will pay to put your home in its current condition and meet all current codes as well), and it typically won't pay to bring your home up to current standards.

Reserve The amount of money set aside by a condo, co-op, or homeowners' association for future capital improvements.

Residual Value How much the car dealer says the car will be worth at the end of the lease term. Typically, this is not negotiable.

Roth IRA The Tax Relief Act of 1997 created a Roth IRA, which allows nondeductible, after-tax contributions of up to $2,000 per year. As long as you hold the IRA for at least five years, the distributions are tax-free. In addition, you are not required to make a minimum contribution each year, and there is no age limit for additional contributions.

Sale-Leaseback A transaction in which the seller sells property to a buyer, who then leases the property back to the seller. This is accomplished within the same transaction.

Sales Contract The document by which a buyer contracts to purchase property. Also known as the *purchase contract* or a *contract to purchase*.

Sales Tax In most areas, a car lease is considered the same as a purchase. So you'll pay sales tax on your purchase.

That's one reason to think carefully about where you purchase or lease your vehicle. You might pay only 7.5 percent sales tax instead of 8.75 percent, depending on where you buy or lease your car. And when you're talking about a $20,000 car, saving 1.25 percent means saving $250.

Savings Bonds   A bond backed by the U.S. government, savings bonds (which come in different series, like EE and HH) can be purchased in small amounts, either directly from a bank, the Treasury Department, or through a broker. They're nontransferable and are not traded, as are other government offerings. In September 1998 the government began selling an inflation-indexed savings bond. The I-bond guarantees that your return will outpace inflation, and is actually based on the rate of inflation plus a fixed rate of return, perhaps 3 to 3.5 percent.

Savings Incentive Match Plan for Employees (SIM-PLE-401[k] or IRA)   A pension plan for employers with 100 or fewer employees (who earn at least $5,000 per year). The employer must match the employee contribution, which is limited to a dollar amount that is indexed for inflation.

Second Mortgage   A mortgage that is obtained after the primary mortgage, and whose rights for repayment are secondary to the first mortgage.

Seller Broker   A broker who has a fiduciary responsibility to the seller. Most brokers are seller brokers, although an increasing number are buyer brokers, who have a fiduciary responsibility to the buyer.

Settlement Statement   A statement that details the monies paid out and received by the buyer and seller at closing.

Shared Appreciation Mortgage   A relatively new mortgage used to help first-time buyers who might not qualify for conventional financing. In a shared appreciation mortgage, the lender offers a below-market interest rate in return for a portion of the profits made by the homeowner when the property is sold. Before entering into a shared appreciation mortgage, be sure to have your real estate attorney review the documentation.

Simplified Employee Pension (SEP-IRA)   This is a type of pension plan used by small businesses. The employer's contributions are excluded from the employee's taxable salary, and may not exceed 15 percent of the employee's salary or the current dollar amount set by the government, whichever is less.

Social Security   Under the Social Security Act of 1935, the government established the Social Security Administration to provide retirement benefits, disability income, and Medicare for working individuals and their spouses.

Special Assessment   An additional charge levied by a condo or co-op board in order to pay for capital improvements or other unforeseen expenses.

Specialty Fund   A mutual fund that specializes in one particular market sector or industry, or even a specific piece of an industry.

Spin-Off   A company may divide itself into several pieces, giving new shares in the company to current shareholders. Your 100 shares of stock in one company may turn into 300 shares if the company divides itself in three ways and rewards stockholders with one share in each new company for each share currently held.

Standard Deduction   If you decide not to itemize your deductions, or if you can't, you may opt for the standard deduction, an amount set by the government and indexed for inflation.

Stock Rights   Your right as a shareholder to purchase new shares, often at a discount. Sometimes you'll see this if you have an account at a savings and loan that announces it intends to go public. Account holders are offered the right to purchase shares of stock in the company before the initial public offering.

Subagent   A broker who brings the buyer to the property. Although subagents would appear to be working for the buyer (a subagent usually ferries around the buyer, showing him or her properties), they are paid by the seller and have a fiduciary responsibility to the seller. Subagency is often confusing to first-time buyers, who think that because the subagent shows them property, the subagent is "their" agent, rather than the seller's.

Subdivision   The division of a large piece of property into several smaller pieces. Usually a developer or a group of developers will build single family or duplex homes of a similar design and cost within one subdivision.

Subvented Lease   A car lease that's subsidized (typically by the auto manufacturer) in order to get rid of a certain kind of car. Subvented leases can be exceptional deals, and they are often the only way that leasing may be cheaper than owning (unless you pay cash, in which case a well-negotiated car purchase will almost certainly be cheaper than any lease you could get).

Surrender Value   See *Cash Surrender Value*.

Tax Audit   A formal examination of your tax return by IRS auditors.

Tax Bracket   A range of income that must pay a certain level of taxes. The higher your income, the higher your tax bracket and the more tax you pay.

Tax Credit   A dollar-for-dollar amount subtracted directly from the taxes you owe.

Tax Deduction   An amount that reduces your gross income. Common deductions include mortgage interest and school loan interest.

Tax Lien   A lien that is attached to property if the owner does not pay his or her real estate taxes or federal income taxes. If overdue property taxes are not paid, the owner's property might be sold at auction for the amount owed in back taxes.

Tax Shelter   Investments entered into for the primary purpose of lowering your tax burden.

Taxable Income   Your gross earnings minus deductions and exclusions.

Tenancy by the Entirety   A type of ownership whereby both the husband and wife each own the complete property. Each spouse has an ownership interest in the property as their marital residence and, as a result, creditors of one spouse cannot force the sale of the home to pay back his or her debts without the other spouse's consent. There are rights of survivorship whereby upon the death of one spouse, the other spouse would immediately inherit the entire property.

Tenants in Common   A type of ownership in which two or more parties have an undivided interest in the property. The owners may or may not have equal shares of ownership, and there are no rights of survivorship. However, each owner retains the right to sell his or her share in the property as he or she sees fit.

Tender Offer   When a company wants to take over another company, it will offer a price per share that is typically above the market price. You will be asked to tender, or surrender, your shares for the higher price. In reality, after the tender offer is made, the market price for your stock will usually go up and match the offer (if it doesn't match the offer, there is some concern in the market that the deal may not go through).

Term (Bonds)   Short-term bonds run up to three years in length. Intermediate bonds are from three to ten years in length. Long-term bonds run up to thirty years in length. Generally, the bonds that pay the highest interest rate are the long-term bonds. However, you'll only earn an extra percentage point or so on your money and have to tie it up for a long period of time. Financial planners say a better bet is to purchase intermediate-term bonds, which are more flexible.

Term (Car Lease)   How long the car lease lasts. Generally, you won't want to get a car lease for longer than three years. Too many things can start to go wrong with a leased car in it's fourth or fifth year, and the likelihood that you'll get some nicks and dings increases.

Title   Refers to the ownership of a particular piece of property.

Title Company   The corporation or company that insures the status of title on real estate (called *title insurance*) at a closing, and may handle other aspects of the real estate closing.

Title Insurance   Insurance that protects the lender and the property owner against losses arising from undisclosed defects or problems with the title to the property.

Total Return   Your total return is your dividends plus the gain or loss in the price of the company's stock. If the stock rises 5 percent and your dividends are 2 percent, your total return is 7 percent.

Transaction Fees   The costs mutual funds incur when they buy and sell shares of stock on the open market.

Treasuries   The federal government offers three types of products to raise money. They are Treasury bills (also known as a *T-bills*), Treasury notes, and Treasury bonds. Uncle Sam uses the money raised from the sale of these three products to pay for social and spending programs. Collectively, this debt is our national debt. It is considered fail-proof, since it is backed by the U.S. government.

Treasury Bills (T-Bills)   These are government-backed securities, with a minimum purchase price of $1,000. They are offered in three-month, six-month, and twelve-month lengths. You buy the T-bill at a discount which, when divided by the effective cost, equals your rate of interest. (So if you purchase a $10,000 T-bill for $9,300, your interest rate is $700 ÷ $9,300 = .08, or 8 percent.) The discount is deposited immediately into your account, and the rest of the face value arrives on the day the bond matures. You have the option of rolling over your T-bill for another period. Since T-bills, like all offerings from the Treasury Department, are backed by the full faith and credit of the U.S. government, they're considered just about the safest investments around.

Trust Account   An account used by brokers and escrow agents, in which funds for another individual are held separately, and not commingled with other funds.

12(b)-1 Fees   These are a mutual fund's marketing expenses. They include everything from printing brochures to picking up the cost of entertaining or compensating brokers who put their clients into the fund.

Umbrella Liability Policy   Insures losses in excess of amounts covered by other liability insurance policies; also protects the insured in many situations not covered by the usual liability polices.

Underwriter   One who underwrites a loan for another. Your lender will have an investor underwrite your loan.

Universal Life Insurance   A flexible premium life insurance policy under which the policyholder may change the death benefit from time to time (with satisfactory evidence of insurability for increases), vary the amount or timing of premium payments, and choose the investment vehicle for his or her premiums. Premiums (less expense charges and commissions) are credited to a policy account from which mortality charges are deducted and to which interest is credited at a rate that may change from time to time.

Variable Interest Rate   An interest rate that rises and falls according to a particular economic indicator, such as Treasury bills.

Viatical Settlement   Payment of a portion of the proceeds from life insurance to an insured who is terminally ill.

Void   A contract or document that is not enforceable.

Voluntary Lien   A lien, such as a mortgage, that a homeowner elects to grant to a lender.

Waiver   The surrender or relinquishment of a particular right, claim, or privilege.

Warrants   Sometimes when you buy preferred stock or bonds of speculative companies, you get a warrant, or the right to buy additional shares of stock at a predetermined price. This sounds great, but the company usually has the right to call in the warrants, forcing you to exercise them (i.e., buy stock at the current price) or receive a few cents for each warrant you hold.

Warranty, Home   A legally binding promise given to the buyer at closing by the seller, generally regarding the condition of the home, property, or other matter.

Wash Sale   If you sell stocks and repurchase them within thirty days prior to or after the sale.

Withholding   An ongoing deduction from your paycheck that is sent by your employer on your behalf to the IRS.

Withholding Allowance   One withholding allowance is available for each personal and dependent exemption that you're entitled to take. You may also take additional exemptions to compensate for deductions and credits you plan to use. You may change your withholding allowances during the year if your income will be higher or lower than you planned.

Wrap Accounts   Your broker might offer to wrap your mutual funds in with other investments you own, and keep an eye out on all of it, for a 1 to 3 percent wrap account fee. Another wrap account is a mutual fund that has no up-front load, but charges a fixed percentage of assets each year to cover the cost of the commission, management, and expenses.

Yield to Call   If interest rates go down, your bond issuer will want to refinance his debt. That means he'll call in your bond as soon as he can. If your bond has five years until the call date, you'll want to calculate the yield to call, since the bond issuer may not let the bond mature.

Yield to Maturity   If you hold your bond until it matures and reinvest every interest payment at the interest rate on your bond, you would end up with your yield to maturity. If you spend your interest payments, or reinvest them at a lower rate (like in a passbook savings account), your yield to maturity will be less. If you invest them at a higher rate, your yield to maturity will be higher.

Zero Coupon Bonds   These bonds pay zero interest throughout the bond term. However, you buy the bond at a steep discount that includes the implied interest rate. For example, a $1,000 bond paying 8 percent might be purchased for $456. At the date of maturity, you'd collect $544 in interest. The Treasury Department offers *zeros* (as they're commonly called), as do municipalities and some corporations.

Zoning   The right of the local municipal government to decide how different areas of the municipality will be used. Zoning ordinances are the laws that govern the use of the land.

Acknowledgments

Writing a book is a pleasure when you have the assistance of many informed sources, able researchers, and eagle-eyed editors. I am grateful for the friendship of my agent, Alice Martell, and my editor, Betsy Rapoport, whose suggestions on the outline proved fruitful. Annik LaFarge's arrival as we were preparing to go to press provided a welcome burst of energy, insight, and organization. My assistant, April Powell, and radio producer, Todd Mark, provided research and background information. Neda Simeonova helped with the final edit. Brian Belfiglio, my publicist at Three Rivers Press, makes magical things happen almost every day.

My family continues to be so supportive of my efforts, and I am thankful they continue to share their stories and insights. Finally, I would like to thank my husband, Sam, world's best real estate attorney and editor, who continues to believe all my wildest dreams will come true.

Index